# A Taste of VirginiaTech

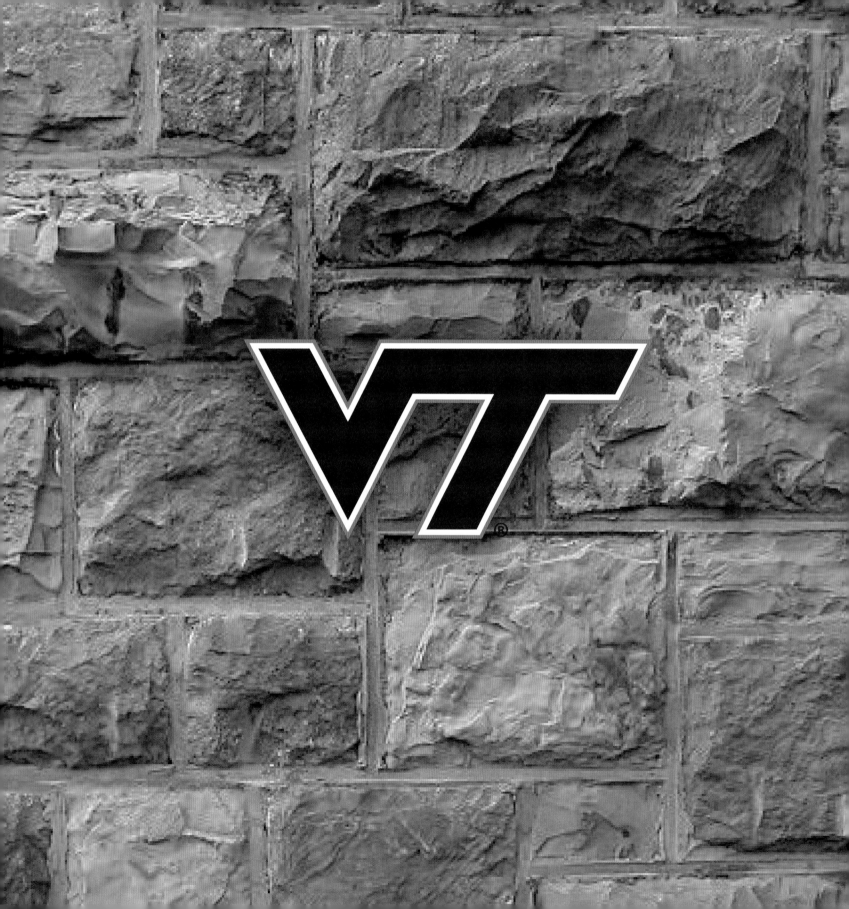

# Contents:

# Introduction

From Krista Gallagher and Kris Schoels

*I* didn't anticipate eating so well in college. When I first set foot in Virginia Tech's West End Market in August 1999, I realized it was not the college dining experience my mom had prepared me for. I was expecting chafing dishes instead of sharp, enameled Dutch ovens, and cutting through unrecognizable meat instead of sizzling hot London broil. I predicted an atmosphere that would make me want to eat and run. Instead, I found one that had me lingering for hours, basking in the rich flavors, hilarious conversation, and, of course, people-watching. Needless to say, I was pleasantly surprised at my beloved school's taste in food.

A couple of years ago, my fellow HighTechs and I sent a string of e-mails titled, "What I would do with one more week at Virginia Tech." I typed up a list of about fifty items that included walking the duck pond, attending dollar pitcher night at the Library, towing one of Tek-Tow's trucks, and so on. While composing this list I realized more than 50 percent of what I wished to experience again revolved around food. Okay, actually 75 percent, but don't you dare judge me. Needless to say, I was unequivocally obsessed with the food from my college days. Two reasons stood out in my mind: first, the food at Virginia Tech is not a joke—it's spectacularly better than most colleges and second, it conjures up so many of my favorite memories of college.

I can link most memories with a specific meal—first dates at Vincent's—penne a la vodka; nursing a hangover at West End—broccoli cheddar soup in a bread bowl; stretching out on the booths at Macado's—chicken parmesan wrap; beginning my Thursday nights at El Rodeo with a jumbo margarita and ending them with a Gumby's pizza—that I can hardly remember, yet never forget. I certainly appreciate most of the dining hall food found on both ends of the drill field. However, I readily admit to being a West End snob. I adore everything about West End Market and still crave it regularly, especially the red-wine-infused marinara sauce that I'd dip the buttery garlic bread in. I love the swirl of activity on Main Street and its long list of multiethnic and unique restaurants. Thoughts of the shrimp and grits at Boudreaux's, chicken pitas at Souvlaki's, and the eggs Florentine at Gillie's still make me ravenous. I'd like to give thanks to the bar named the Library, not only for its dollar pitcher nights, but for providing me with a great answer when my mom asked where I was going that night. She was always proud to hear that I was spending my Wednesday nights at the "Library." Sharkey's wings are still incredible, especially the spicy garlic. The last time I had Sharkey's wings as a student I was supposed to be fasting for a cholesterol test for a class assignment. Needless to say, my usual below-normal cholesterol was off the charts and it was worth every bit of LDL. The food at Virginia Tech, whether on or off campus, is comforting, soulful, and evokes enough strong memories to last a lifetime.

*Whenever I go back for football games, I always end up at Top of the Stairs and ultimately get—what else—the Rail. Any hangover could easily be traced back to this drink, couldn't it? One night toward the end of my senior year, a few of us went to TOTS for an early dinner. We sat at the bar and ordered grilled cheese sandwiches. We looked at each other, then back at the bartender, and said, "…and a Rail." My favorite TOTS moment came on Valentine's Day in 2003. With no explanation necessary, my friend Mich and I decided to hit up the bars early. Off we went to TOTS where I spotted a really good-looking guy and wished him a happy "singles awareness day." Three-and-a-half years later, he became my husband. If you can't find romance at TOTS, where can you? Top of the Stairs will always hold a special place in my heart.*

*The idea for this cookbook came to me one day as I was driving and thinking about what I could do with my passion for cooking. The* Princeton Review *named Virginia Tech number one for best campus food in 2008 and my quest to understand Virginia Tech's culinary success had begun. The conversations I had with Tech fans solidified my belief that the food at Virginia Tech is special. I suddenly felt compelled to write about another reason to be proud of our great school. When I began my research, I was blown away by the dramatic transformation that campus dining has undergone. There was a real story there and it needed to be told.*

*I sat down with the creators of West End Market and learned it was just as much the quality of the people as the food that made this "fab" dining hall such a hit. I was inspired by Dr. Spencer and Rick Johnson's story. Their team took a novel approach to campus dining and transformed it into a successful business, while giving college students something they'd never experienced before: really delicious food. I sat in awe as they told me their plans for a dining hall opening in 2012 in the academic part of campus, just behind McBride. Sushi? A crêperie? An espresso bar? Gelato? I think I'll have to enroll in a postgraduate program.*

*My fellow Hokie lovers, enjoy this culinary adventure through Virginia Tech. If you're a student, show your families and friends from other schools just how spoiled you are and remember to savor the memories while you can. If you're an alumnus, enjoy reminiscing about the food from your college days and learning how your alma mater has evolved. If you didn't get to experience the fabulous West End Market, this is an opportunity to experience it in your own home. So, cleanse your palate for* A Taste of Virginia Tech.

*-Krista Gallagher*

When Krista asked me to join her on a culinary journey culminating in a cookbook titled A Taste of Virginia Tech, I didn't hesitate before saying yes. It's always been hard for me to explain to those who didn't go to Virginia Tech exactly what the school means to me and thousands of other alumni.

How do you explain to someone the thrill of hearing the gobbling scoreboard at football games and the sleepless nights spent camping outside for student football tickets? Are there enough words to describe the sights, smells, and sounds of tailgating that begin a week before the game and don't end until the day after? Can someone who never went to Tech truly understand the colors on campus in the height of fall, the bitter cold of winter spent walking across the drill field, or the flowers blooming at the duck pond in the spring?

How do you truly explain what a being a Hokie means?

A Hokie is bonding with friends over West End's London broil, meeting a study group at Deet's Place for unbelievable ice cream, or hitting up Owens for a smoothie with friends.

A Hokie is Tuesday Karaoke at TOTS, Rail in hand, Thursday night socials at El Rodeo, pool tournaments at Hokie House, and dancing at that place whose name has changed 50 times since the school opened.

A Hokie is a gigantic turkey drumstick at a tailgate and the smell of burgers being cooked on the flatbed of a pickup truck.

A Hokie is laughter, painted faces, a rush of maroon and orange, and the Hokie Pokie being danced in the stands.

A Hokie is PK's pizza, homemade pasta at The Cellar, burgers at Mike's, late night breakfast at Joe's Diner, and pokey stix from Gumby's, shared with friends at 3 a.m.

The point is, you can't fully explain to someone what being a Hokie means. They have to feel it for themselves. However, Krista and I hope that you can give non-Hokies at least a taste of the experience.

Join us on the journey that is A Taste of Virginia Tech. When you share the recipes in this book with your loved ones, you're sharing a bit of what it means to be a Hokie.

-Kris Schoels

# From Mystery Meat to Fresh Maine Lobster:

## The Evolution of the Dining Hall Experience at Virginia Tech

G one are the days when students had to point at a lump of unrecognizable food and say, "I'll take some of that." At Virginia Tech, the dark and dingy dining hall is a thing of the past. Reform of on-campus dining at Virginia Tech took decades, as well as countless vocal, discontented students, and a dining department full of pioneers. The result has been simply revolutionary.

Established as a military institute, it is not surprising that Virginia Tech's only dining facility existed as a typical mess hall. Not just a clever name, it was indeed a hot "mess." Referring to the main course as "mystery meat" is neither untrue nor unkind. Growley was the official nickname of the aforementioned mystery meat, which was scraps of leftover meat (usually turkey) and bones that had been ground together. Yuck.

In 1940, Virginia Tech's first traditional dining facility opened and was later named Owens Dining Hall for former mess steward John Joseph Owens. Owens, who served 1917–1940, was affectionately called Pop. He became a confidant and friend to his cadets, and was fondly remembered for hosting an annual Thanksgiving dinner.[1] Owens advocated for higher quality and was ultimately the driving force behind initial improvements to Virginia Tech's dining.

During the 1960s, a dramatic increase in student population, voluntary participation from the corps of cadets, and shifting culinary trends prompted changes to campus dining at Virginia Tech. In 1962, Shultz Dining Hall opened. Nestled in the upper quadrangle of the campus, Shultz accommodated the influx of students as it had the capacity to serve a little more than 2,000 cadets at a time. It was Virginia Tech's first "specialty" dining center where students could eat a larger variety of foods than at Owens Hall. Although Shultz was not a complete failure, students remained repulsed by what they considered deplorable food at all three dining halls. Student-led smear campaigns, protests, and boycotts of the halls garnered attention from the local media. In a Roanoke Times article dated November 1, 1961, a former manager of Owens stated that although some complaints were justified, "We can't serve meals as tasty as mother makes them." Students wondered why not.

The frustration at the inability to get a decent meal on campus mounted and led to students petitioning the school's administration. They used surveys to solicit negative opinions about the dining halls and also formed

organizations such as BARF (Back the Attack on Repugnant Food). These tactics created enough pressure to trigger the first of two renovations of Owens Dining Hall, which has indeed come a long way. Today, Owens Food Court boasts 12 specialty shops, ranging from America's favorite comfort foods to internationally inspired markets, organic produce, grass-fed beef, and the wildly popular frozen yogurt machine.

By the late 1960s, the food court concept became popular. In 1970, one of the nation's largest dining halls, Dietrick, named for Dean of Agriculture Leander B. Dietrick, was opened. Located on the residential side of campus, Dietrick Hall was not only convenient, but a place where you could bring your appetite. Many students, especially the football team, appreciated its simple, all-you-can-eat, traditional food. Dietrick Hall was the first dining facility in Virginia Tech's history to take advantage of the bountiful produce from the farmlands of Blacksburg, by adding fresh vegetables (as opposed to canned) to the menu. However, while the addition of Dietrick Dining Hall was a welcome one, students still wanted more.

The real changes came in the fall of 1988 when Jim McComas became president of Virginia Tech. McComas was strongly focused on improving students' quality of life and therefore made the decision to reposition Dining Services under the Division of Student Affairs. He asked a question of the then director of housing and residence life, Dr. Edward Spencer, "Do you think we can turn this dining program into something we can be proud of?"

Dr. Spencer felt empowered by the challenge to become director of residential and dining programs and transform dining on campus, so he sought out Paul Fairbrook, retired dean of the Culinary Institute of America, for consultation. Fairbrook stayed for six months and sparked several changes from requiring the servers to wear white gloves to using cooking thermometers.

In 1991, Owens Dining Hall underwent a second transformation. A portion of the building was sectioned off to create another dining hall and the student-named Hokie Grill was born. Two years later, Spencer hired Rick Johnson as the director of Dining Services, and on-campus dining

improvements took off. What set Johnson apart was that instead of just studying what other universities did, he sought inspiration from top restaurants across the nation. "We wanted to become more retail oriented, like a restaurant," Johnson said. "So our goal was to revolutionize the way we thought about food and service."

Johnson put a 10-year plan into action. Part of the plan included placing ultrapopular national brands such as Chick-fil-A, Cinnabon, and Pizza Hut in Hokie Grill. However, because it was not economically feasible to offer high quality food at an all-you-can-eat price, Johnson's team recognized that it would be next to impossible to bring these foods to campus without adapting the existing meal plan. As a result, dining services added a flexible spending, or flex plan, which functioned as a debit card to allow students to purchase items a la carte. Students quickly saw the value in the new plan and its popularity skyrocketed and so did Hokie Grill's. The idea of bringing popular franchises onto campus proved to be an effective strategy for increasing revenue and keeping current students happy and future students excited for a small piece of familiarity in alien territory.

Possibly the strongest testament of the flex plan's success is this: when students move off campus, it is not required that they hold a meal plan. Yet interestingly, thousands still prefer to eat on campus. That's how good the food is. Today, there are over 9,700 off-campus (or optional) meal plan holders and 9,100 on-campus holders, making Virginia Tech's dining program the largest in the nation.

The flex plan afforded Virginia Tech's dining program many opportunities including the creation of a new facility that would later propel the university to a completely different level in food service: one of excellence. In January 1999, Virginia Tech unveiled its premier dining hall—the West End Market—named for its marketplace style and its location at the west end of campus. The university has received numerous accolades for the unique concept of West End and the students rave about its delicious food, which includes fresh seafood, house-made soups, a wide selection of made-to-order burgers, and even whole lobsters. West End may very well be some students' first taste of the sea's most revered product.

By the late 1990s, each major dining hall underwent vast restoration with the exception of Dietrick Hall. Dietrick's positive reputation plummeted after the airing of a 2004 show entitled Dirty Dining, which featured employees engaging in unsanitary practices while handling food. As a result, the upper portion of Dietrick Hall underwent serious renovation and was renamed D2. The new eatery is as cool as its name suggests and adds spice to the campus with its market style and sharp décor. Bright and modern pendant lights add flare to this internationally inspired dining hall. At D2, students nosh on a large variety of foods at each market, including skewered meats at Gauchos - a Brazilian churrascaria, a "VT"-embossed Belgian waffle at La Pâtisserie, and even vegan cuisine at Olives.

The lower level of Dietrick is home to Deet's Place, a whimsical coffee and ice cream shop with plenty of space for students to study and, of course, socialize. Deet's hand-dipped milkshakes, sparkling Italian sodas, and creamy lattes all make study time a more enjoyable experience.

The year 2012 will be a proud one for Virginia Tech, with the addition of Turner Place, a state-of-the-art dining facility strategically located on the academic side of campus. Inspired by student feedback, Turner Place will conveniently allow students and faculty to grab a meal or snack in between classes, but it will not serve just any campus food. This dining hall is going to set a new standard as VT students are used to being spoiled with fine cuisine. It will feature a crêperie, an espresso bar, house-made gelato, a Japanese steakhouse, and national brands such as Jamba Juice, Qdoba, and Bruegger's Bagels. This ultramodern venue will seat 700 and include a separate dining room for the corps of cadets. As Frank Shushok, associate vice president for student affairs, says, "In addition to great food, Turner Place will bring together faculty, staff, and students around the dining table, strengthening our community of friendship and learning and energizing campus life in the academic corridor." [2]

Virginia Tech's culinary victory stems from passion, extraordinary leadership, teamwork, and impeccable attention to detail. Now that it has seen the rewards of overhauling the status quo of campus dining, the Department of Student Affairs has vowed to never rest on its laurels. Instead of being satisfied with one very successful dining hall (West End Market), the Department of Student Affairs made it their mission to produce far-reaching improvements to all other dining halls, keeping the cuisine inventive and fun. That is why Virginia Tech has received national recognition, including the Princeton Review's number-one rank for best campus food in both 2008 and 2010. In fact, the university has been ranked in the top three by the Princeton Review for best campus food for the past ten years. This honor is perhaps Virginia Tech's proudest achievement, albeit not a scientific ranking (it's based on customer/student feedback) it was exactly what Virginia Tech wanted: happy students.

Improvements took the better part of a century, and now there is no mystery meat to be found on Virginia Tech's campus. In fact, Virginia Tech students say these dining halls serve meals "better" than mother makes them.

[1]Virginia Tech website, "About Virginia Tech Buildings" para. 5          [2]Virginia Tech website, "About Virginia Tech Buildings" para. 6

West End Market's
Executive Chef
Mark Bratton

# West End Market:

Game Changer in Campus Dining

*C*ollege and good food—those words had never before shared a sentence, until *Virginia Tech* decided it was time to create a paradigm shift in the lifestyles of so-called starving college students. The university doesn't just stay on top of food trends; it creates them. It is at the cutting edge of haute cuisine and other colleges across the country are paying attention.

West End Market, Virginia Tech's innovative and illustrious dining hall, shoved traditional campus dining aside—out with the chafing dishes and in with the freshly made, piping hot lobster bisque. Introduced in 1999, West End Market is self-operated, which means it hasn't been subcontracted to a large company, which is often attractive to smaller schools because they can provide food services at much lower prices. However, self-operation affords West End Market greater autonomy to control all elements of the business, including style and design as well as menu and chef selection. This ownership results in a restaurant-like dining experience where high quality, not cost containment, is the number-one priority.

In 1993, when Rick Johnson became director of Culinary Services, the hallmark of dining halls across the nation was an all-you-can-eat selection of traditional foods. However, food courts were gaining popularity because they offered a greater variety of dishes, many of which were produced on a made-to-order basis. Virginia Tech's Owens Food Court, whose lines flowed out of the building and had to be controlled at the door, made it clear that students preferred the food court to the traditional style of dining.

Aware of the escalating popularity of Owens Food Court, Johnson pressed students for feedback in an effort to understand what they wanted. He was determined to more effectively improve dining on campus. The students' opinions were unanimous: they craved affordable, restaurant quality, reminiscent of home-cooking, and comfort foods. Within that first year, Johnson's team, which included associates John Price, Ted Faulkner, Robert Coffey, and Brian Grove, created a vision that they believed would propel dining services to a whole new level.

Thanks to the revenue generated by the flex dining plan, the Department of Dining Services was given free rein to develop West End Market. In 1997, the new dining hall was built, strategically placed on the residential side of campus and attached to Cochrane Residence Hall. Its hallmark feature, the market, quickly became the most unique take on a college dining hall to date.

"The marketplace concept had not yet come into vogue," Johnson said. "Not even commercially, let alone on a college campus, so we were doing something that had never been done before." Johnson's team drew inspiration from and consulted with two marketplace dining establishments, Toronto's Le Marché and Chicago's Foodlife, both of which had pioneered this incredibly successful style of dining. These marketplaces have great vibrancy and an impressive variety of cuisine because they host numerous restaurants in one arena. This approach offers the advantage of freshly made foods done in small batches, which ensures higher quality compared to a traditional selection. It was a different, fun way to dine—and Johnson's team wanted to make it work at Virginia Tech.

Since the marketplace was a new concept and relatively untried, Johnson needed buy-in from the students. He formed a student focus group and flew them to Chicago via the Hokie Bird jet to show them firsthand why he was so excited about bringing a market to Virginia Tech's campus. Johnson said he would never forget one student's remarks during the trip. Referring to the future West End Market, the student said, "If it can be anything like this, it will be the greatest thing we've ever done at Virginia Tech."

As far as food goes, it was. West End is comprised of six marketplaces, which enable students to indulge in a variety of dishes. Large stockpots of simmering pasta sauces at Bistro Firenze, a creamy cheesecake of the day at Wired, the top selling Hokie club at the Cutting Edge, juicy burgers at the Fighting Gobbler, and the famous London broil with garlic whipped potatoes at JP's Chophouse all make the possibilities at West End seem endless. West End even offers steamed Maine lobster. That's right, lobster.

Beyond creating a fun epicurean experience, West End Market has proved to be a lucrative business for the university. In its first year, West End exceeded its revenue goals threefold and its revenue for 2010 was an incredible $8.5 million. In addition to its financial success, West End has received numerous accolades for its concept and design. Although not the sole reason, its popularity certainly contributed to Virginia Tech winning both the Princeton Review's number-one rank for best campus food and the prestigious Ivy award (given by Restaurants and Institutions Magazine to the top five restaurants in the country). Much of West End's success is attributed, in part, to Head Chef Mark Bratton's perfectionism and leadership, which shines through every dish that's prepared.

Virginia Tech identified a need for higher quality food on campus and more importantly, made it happen. In return, student satisfaction improved and Virginia Tech reaped handsome rewards in both revenue and marketability.

Note: Good news for alumni who graduated prior to West End's opening: You don't need a Hokie passport to dine at West End Market. You can purchase a dining card with cash at the machine right as you walk in or you can simply use a credit card. So next time you're in town, pay a visit to West End Market to fully understand why the Virginia Tech dining experience is all the rage.

# Gourmet Pantry

*I*t's impossible to leave Gourmet Pantry without feeling happy. Owner Roya Gharavi has created an inviting, modern environment that beckons one to indulge. Phrases like, "Yeah right, this is awesome," "OMG, I need this," and "Stop it right now—this is amazing" were uttered multiple times during our visit. We're not being dramatic here. We city girls were stunned that our beloved college town would have a kitchen supply store so complete and so beautiful.

When we first stepped inside, we were immediately drawn to a huge, granite-topped island lined with bar stools behind a sparkling Viking range. It was so homey; we instantly wanted to sit down and watch someone cook. We fought the urge because of all the serious browsing we had to do. The store's items range from very basic (measuring cups, spatulas) to specialty (soda stream machine, juicers) to fine foods (aged balsamic, chia seeds, chocolate). Gourmet Pantry's supply is much more extensive than we'd ever imagined. Much of Gharavi's success is in staying ahead of the trends in both food and equipment. The store and, more importantly, Gharavi, has ignited a passion for food and cooking in Blacksburg.

Inspired by the lack of both specialty and basic kitchenware stores in Blacksburg, self-taught cook Gharavi opened perhaps the neatest shop downtown. In 2000, Gourmet Pantry opened its doors to fulfill this need, which was timely, given the residents' growing interest in agriculture and all things culinary.

You would never know Gharavi wasn't a classically trained chef. She has an impressive knowledge of cooking thanks to her tenure in the restaurant business, owning her first restaurant in Virginia Beach at the tender age of 21, the guidance of various mentors, and studying the sixth edition of the Culinary Institute of America's cookbook. Gharavi has been a fixture in Blacksburg since the 1990s and has had a remarkable influence on its culinary culture.

Gharavi first entered the Blacksburg culinary scene by opening Champions Pizza, which later moved and morphed into the still-popular Champs Sports Bar and Catering. After eight successful years, she sold Champs and opened Gourmet Pantry on South Main Street. Gharavi dreamed of someday opening a cooking school and the store quickly outgrew its original space, so Gourmet Pantry subsequently moved into a newly constructed ground location on North Main Street and was reinvented as the Gourmet Pantry and Cooking School. Gharavi's mission in her classes is to "teach people at all comfort levels how to cook and eat healthy foods." She accomplishes that in each class, sharing both her passion for cooking and confidence in her skills with her audience.

The cooking school has taken off, offering classes on such subjects as healthy Mediterranean cuisine, knife skills, tailgating, sushi, and cupcakes. Gharavi subscribes to Blacksburg's own food philosophy: be local, buy local, eat local. Most of the ingredients she uses in her classes are purchased at the local farmers' market, which benefits the community as well as the environment.

When we asked what she wanted Gourmet Pantry's legacy to be, Gharavi humbly said, "Quality products, excellent customer service, and seeing our customers walk out genuinely happy." So three chocolate bars, a Virginia Tech cake pan, cooking scale, jar of chia seeds, a wonderful conversation, and a balsamic vinegar tasting later, we agreed that Gharavi and Gourmet Pantry had exceeded all our expectations as well as hers. For more information and a calendar of cooking classes, go to www.gourmetpantryonline.com.

# Blacksburg:

## Support of the Local Food Movement

# Buy Local. Eat Local. Live Local.

O n an off-day, you may have wandered by the empty park that houses the Blacksburg Farmers'
Market and not even realized how, on Saturday mornings, that spot comes to life. When we visited
Blacksburg in August 2011, it was abuzz with activity. Vendors lined the concrete stalls and people
were practically pushing past each other for produce (or maybe that was us trying to get the last cinnamon roll).
Nevertheless, the smell of freshly baked donuts and the aforementioned rolls wafted through the warm air and
begged us to take a closer look. We spied a sign for gluten-free goodies, and wondered, where are we?

Perhaps we hadn't given enough credit to our small college town, but we were impressed that the local
vendors kept in vogue with the latest food trends. The size of this year-round market is generous and its energy
electric. It boasts more seasonal fruits, vegetables, and baked goods vendors than you can count on both hands.
Locally sourced ingredients are used to create pies, scones, granola, breads, and honey, all of which added to
the whimsical farmers' market experience.

The Blackburg Farmers' Market started up in the '80s with farmers selling goods from their vehicles
in a strip-mall parking lot on South Main Street. In 1996, the town and downtown merchants of Blacksburg
came together to build a structure for the market, and it has since been revamped and renamed. Market
Square Park was officially finished in December 2009.

The market has even become popular among Virginia Tech students. Our student intern Christina
Wingfield has developed a Saturday morning obsession with the market and raves about the blackberry jam
and goat cheese crêpes made on-site. Purveyors of the market are local restaurant owners, hand picking many
of their ingredients for special recipes.

It is obvious that the market's vendors are passionate about the high quality products they are selling
and are on the cutting edge of the latest food news and trends, thus increasing the market's popularity among
residents and students alike.

Another vision of the local food movement is quite evident in the "Farms and Fields" program that was implemented in January 2009 in Owens Food Court. It incorporates products from local farmers and the university's own Kentland Farm in order to provide a local and sustainable food option to students. The garden is a collaboration between dining services and the College of Agriculture and Life Sciences. In the last year alone, "Farms and Fields" has sustained nearly two acres of vegetable and herb production, tested over 150 recipes, and most importantly, introduced ice cream from the local Homestead Creamery. We've heard it's to live for.

This is yet another example of how Blacksburg and Virginia Tech are on point with all the latest food trends: local, sustainable, and organic.

*The Blacksburg Farmers' Market is open year round. For more information, go to*

## *www.blacksburgfarmersmarket.com.*

# Appetizers

Souvlaki's Tiropita

The Cellar's Cajun Shrimp Dip

The Cellar's Tzatziki Sauce

622 North's Seared Mahi with Mango Slaw

Pita Vera's Balila

Backstreets' Fried Mushrooms

Backstreets' Buffalo Chicken Strips

Poor Billy's Gorgonzola Mussels

Poor Billy's Tuna with Tomato and Blue Crab Anisette

Zeppoli's Spinach and Artichoke Dip

Zeppoli's Garlic Butter

Café de Bangkok's Chicken Satay and Peanut Sauce

Deet's Place Sundried Tomato Dip

Poor Billy's
Gorgonzola Mussels
Pg. 36

# Souvlaki's
## Tiropita

*This recipe was created by Maria Kappas, the wife of Souvlaki's original owner. Here's a tip for using phyllo dough: it dries out quickly so work with two strips at a time or use the premade phyllo cups found in the freezer section of your grocery store. Both options taste great.*

Serves 6–8

8 ounces feta cheese
8 ounces ricotta cheese
1 (8-ounce) package cream cheese, softened
½ teaspoon white pepper
3 eggs plus 2 egg yolks
½ pound phyllo dough
½ to ¾ pound butter, melted
sesame seeds, for garnish

Preheat oven to 350°F.

Crumble feta cheese into small pieces in a large bowl. Add ricotta, cream cheese, white pepper, and eggs, and stir until well blended.

Cut sheets of phyllo into 3-inch strips and brush with melted butter. Spoon 1 teaspoon of cheese mixture on the end of strip and fold into triangles.

Place triangles on a greased baking sheet, brush each triangle with more melted butter, and sprinkle with sesame seeds. Bake for 20–30 minutes or until golden brown. Serve hot.

Souvlaki's started out as a food cart in downtown Blacksburg and in 1987, moved to a small storefront with just seven stools at the counter and only five items on the menu. When owner, Chris Kappas, noticed that people seemed perplexed by the menu items that were "not hotdogs and French fries," he began offering samples of his dishes on toothpicks and Souvlaki's popularity soared. According to Kappas, Souvlaki's "literally sold our business on a toothpick." Since then, the restaurant has been taken over by Mike "the Boss" Buchanon and remains one of the most popular places to stop on Main Street.

# The Cellar's
# Cajun Shrimp Dip

*The Cellar is inarguably one of the best date spots and this appetizer certainly heats things up. Feel free to increase the amount of spices to your liking. This dip can be stored in an airtight container in the refrigerator for up to five days.*

Serves 6

1 pound popcorn shrimp*
8 tablespoons unsalted butter
1 teaspoon cayenne pepper
1 teaspoon paprika
1 teaspoon crushed red pepper flakes
2 (8-ounce) packages cream cheese, at room temperature
1 cup ricotta cheese
2 tablespoons Parmesan or Romano cheese
salt, to taste

Rinse shrimp and blot dry with paper towels.

Melt butter in a large skillet on medium heat. Add shrimp, cayenne, paprika, and red pepper flakes, and sauté until pink, about 2 minutes.

With a wooden spoon, add chunks of cream cheese. Lower heat to low, cover, and cook until cream cheese is melted, stirring occasionally. Add ricotta and Parmesan, and whip vigorously until smooth.

Pour into a bowl and serve hot with tortilla chips or pita bread.

*Look for a bag of shrimp with a count of 150–200.

The restaurant with the greatest longevity (and possible haunting) is what is now known as The Cellar, originally called the Blue Ribbon Café. Nick Kappas, a first-generation Greek immigrant, opened the Blue Ribbon Café in the 1920s and featured authentic Greek and Italian cuisine. It soon became so popular patrons gave the restaurant the nickname, the Greek's Place. During the 1960s, the Havelos, another Greek family, joined the business, but ultimately both families parted ways, with one family reopening The Greek's Place in a new location and the other opening Souvlaki's.

In 1963, the basement level of the café opened up and was named, of course, The Cellar. In 1986, current owner Kevin Long purchased The Cellar and committed to keeping the tradition for hearty Greek and Italian fare alive. Known for its calzones, tzatziki, and romantic atmosphere, The Cellar is the place to go when you have a hot date. And if conversation is lacking with said hot date, bring up the rumblings of the restaurant being haunted by ghosts: employees occasionally hearing laughter, plates flying off the shelves, and taps turning on simultaneously by themselves.

In 2011, a new section of the restaurant, The Cellar 6-Pak, opened. It's home to an impressive array of domestic and imported beers, deli meats, and desserts.

# The Cellar's
# Tzatziki Sauce

*Start to make this two days before you plan on serving it as the cucumbers need to marinate for optimal flavor. It is recommended to serve this sauce alongside pita chips or grilled chicken, but no one will judge you if you eat it by the spoonful instead.*

Serves 4–6

3 cucumbers, large diced
1 tablespoon minced garlic
¼ cup freshly squeezed lemon juice
⅛ cup red wine vinegar
1 teaspoon fresh dill, finely chopped
1 teaspoon fresh mint, finely chopped
Kosher salt and black pepper, to taste
1 quart sour cream

Place cucumber chunks in a food processor until coarsely shredded. Pour into a colander to drain and squeeze out excess juice with your hands.

Place the shredded cucumbers in a container and add minced garlic, lemon juice, red wine vinegar, dill, and mint. Season with 1-2 pinches of salt and pepper. Stir to combine. Cover and refrigerate for 2 days.

When ready to serve, add a quart of sour cream to cucumber mixture and stir to combine. Add salt and pepper to taste. Serve with pita bread, chicken, pork, or any spicy dish.

Appetizers  30

# 622 North's
# Seared Mahi with Mango Slaw

*This slaw is filled with so many fresh flavors from the mangos that we had a hard time letting it sit in the fridge for 20 minutes before dipping into it with a fork.*

Serves 6–8

4 mangos, small diced
½ medium red onion, thinly sliced
½ head cabbage, thinly sliced
¼ cup chopped fresh cilantro, plus extra for garnish
1 cup white vinegar
½ cup orange juice
½ cup sugar
1 teaspoon crushed red pepper
salt and pepper, to taste
2 (8-ounce) mahi filets
olive oil

Mix half of the diced mango with onion, cabbage, cilantro, vinegar, ¼ cup orange juice, ¼ cup sugar, and red pepper in a medium bowl. Stir well and season with salt and pepper. Let sit in the refrigerator for 20 minutes.

Heat remaining mango, sugar, and orange juice in a small saucepan on medium-high heat for 8–10 minutes until fruit is very soft. Puree mixture using blender, food processor, or immersion blender, adding orange juice until you reach desired consistency—it should be fairly thin. Set aside.

Season fish with salt and pepper. Heat a small amount of olive oil in a skillet on medium-high heat and sauté fish for 2–3 minutes on each side. Remove from pan and cut into small pieces.

Serve mahi over mango slaw, drizzled with mango sauce. Garnish with cilantro sprigs.

*Pita Vera's*
# Balila

*If you are looking for healthy foods without sacrificing great taste, come to Pita Vera. Even a local doctor sends his patients here to better their diet. We had a blast dining at this relatively new Lebanese restaurant, chatting it up with owner, George, and shoveling copious amounts of these flavorful garbanzo beans into our mouths.*

Serves 6-8

1 (16-ounce) can garbanzo beans
1 clove garlic, minced
pinch of salt
pinch of cumin
2 tablespoons freshly squeezed lemon juice
1 teaspoon olive oil
diced tomatoes and onions, for garnish
chopped fresh parsley, for garnish

Drain the can of garbanzo beans and rinse with cold water. Place the beans in a saucepan and cover with water. Bring to a boil and let cook for 10 minutes.

Meanwhile, smash together garlic and salt until smooth. Whisk together the smashed garlic, cumin, lemon juice, and olive oil in a medium bowl.

Add the garbanzo beans to the dressing and stir to coat. Top with tomatoes, onions, and parsley right before serving.

# Backstreets'
# Fried Mushrooms

*Backstreets is another fine example of how important loyal patrons are to local businesses here. This restaurant has serviced the town since 1984, when it was located on a back street in downtown Blacksburg.*

Serves 2–4

4 eggs
2 cups milk
1 cup flour
4 cups panko bread crumbs
¼ cup Parmesan cheese
1 tablespoon grated Romano cheese
1 teaspoon chopped fresh parsley
½ teaspoon garlic powder
dash each of salt and pepper
2 portabella mushroom caps, each cut into 6 slices
vegetable oil, for frying
marinara sauce, for dipping

Set out three, clean, medium bowls. Whisk together the eggs and milk in the first bowl. Place flour in the second bowl. Combine breadcrumbs, both cheeses, parsley, garlic powder, salt, and pepper in the last bowl.

Place sliced mushrooms in the egg wash and let sit for 2 minutes. Remove mushrooms from the egg wash with a fork or slotted spoon and dredge in flour until well coated. Return mushrooms to egg wash until flour coating is saturated, about 1–2 minutes more.

Working one slice at a time, place mushrooms in breadcrumb mixture and press lightly to coat. Transfer to a clean plate until ready to fry. Repeat with remaining slices.

Pour oil to a depth of 2 inches in a medium saucepan and heat on medium-high heat. Bring oil to 300°F. Working in batches, fry only 3–4 slices at a time until a medium golden brown color, about 2 minutes on each side. Remove with a slotted spoon and place on a plate lined with a paper towel. Repeat with remaining mushrooms.

Serve hot with marinara sauce.

# Backstreets'
# Buffalo Chicken Strips

*These are great for game day. Hot, spicy, and delicious.*

Serves 2–4

2 cups hot sauce
¼ cup unsalted butter, melted
2 tablespoons flour
1 cup flour
2 (6-ounce) chicken breasts, each cut into 4 strips
vegetable oil, for frying
ranch or bleu cheese dressing, for dipping

Combine hot sauce, melted butter, and 2 tablespoons flour in a medium bowl. Place 1 cup of flour in another bowl. Place chicken in the hot sauce mixture and let stand for 2 minutes. Remove chicken from the hot sauce and dredge in bowl of flour until well coated.

Pour vegetable oil to a depth of 2 inches in a medium saucepan and heat on medium-high heat. Bring oil to 300°F. Working in batches, carefully place 3–4 pieces of chicken into the oil and cook until they are a deep golden brown, about 2–3 minutes on each side. Remove with a slotted spoon and place on a plate lined with a paper towel. Repeat with remaining chicken.

Serve with dressing on the side.

# Poor Billy's
# Gorgonzola Mussels

*We highly recommend this recipe. It was one of our favorite recipes tested while writing this book. Poor Billy's is loved for its seafood and sushi. The restaurant recently expanded its business by opening Poor Billy's Small Plates.*

Serves 2

30 icy-blue mussels
2 tablespoons unsalted butter
1 tablespoon minced garlic
⅛ cup chopped green onion
⅛ cup chopped fresh parsley
1 cup white wine
1 cup vegetable or chicken stock
½ teaspoon salt
1½ cups crumbled Gorgonzola cheese
small toasted baguette, for dipping

Clean mussels by scrubbing, rinsing, and removing beards; set aside. Melt butter in a 4-quart saucepan or stockpot over medium heat. Add garlic and stir until it begins to lightly brown. Add the chopped green onions and parsley and cook for 30 seconds.

Pour white wine, stock, and salt into the pot and bring to a boil. Add the cleaned mussels, cover, agitate the pot by shaking briefly and cook for 4 minutes. Sprinkle the crumbled Gorgonzola over the top of the mussels, cover, and cook for an additional minute.

Pour into large bowls and serve with toasted baguette.

# Poor Billy's
# Tuna with Tomato and Blue Crab Anisette

*If you want good seafood in Blacksburg, go to Poor Billy's. This dish is fresh and flavorful. We ate so much of it we considered listing it as a main dish.*

Serves 2–4

vegetable oil, for searing
2 (6 to 8-ounce) tuna steaks
2 teaspoons vegetable oil
1 teaspoon minced garlic
1 teaspoon chopped fennel fronds or tarragon
¾ cup diced tomatoes
4 ounces blue crab meat
¼ cup anisette liqueur
½ cup white wine
salt and pepper, to taste
2 tablespoons unsalted butter

Heat a small amount of vegetable oil in a large skillet on high heat. Season tuna steaks with salt and pepper. Sear tuna to your desired temperature. Remove from pan and place on a clean plate. Cover to keep warm.

Using the same skillet, warm 2 teaspoons vegetable oil on medium-low heat and add minced garlic. Stir until garlic is cooked, 1–2 minutes. Add the chopped herbs, tomatoes, and crab meat. Add the liquor, raise the heat, bring to a simmer, and carefully flambé the liquor.

Add the white wine once the liquor has burned off. Reduce liquid by half and season with salt and pepper. Remove from heat, add the butter, and stir until melted.

Top tuna with crab sauce and serve.

# Zeppoli's
# Spinach and Artichoke Dip

*This bread bowl of cheesy, creamy deliciousness is perfect for entertaining a large group, or great for two people just sitting around on the couch on a rainy Saturday afternoon. Whoops!*

Serves 4–6

½ cup mayonnaise
8 ounces cream cheese, softened
¾ cup grated Parmesan cheese
2 tablespoons lemon juice
1 tablespoon chopped red onion
1 clove garlic, minced
2 (14-ounce) cans artichoke hearts, drained and chopped
4 ounces fresh spinach, chopped
1 large round bread loaf
½ cup shredded mozzarella cheese

Preheat oven to 400°F.

Combine the mayonnaise and cream cheese in a large bowl and stir until smooth. Add the Parmesan cheese, lemon juice, red onion, and garlic, and mix well. Fold in the artichoke hearts and chopped spinach.

Cut the top off of the bread loaf and hollow it out, making a bowl shape and leaving a 1-inch wall all the way around.

Place bread loaf on baking pan and cut the top into 6 wedges and place around the bread bowl. Fill bread bowl with the artichoke mixture and top with mozzarella cheese.

Bake for approximately 25–30 minutes until filling is hot and cheese is melted and bubbly.

Zeppoli's Restaurant and Wine Shop, opened in 1996, is locally owned and operated by Doris Fleming. Drawing from recipes handed down by her Italian relatives and recipes she had created while working in the food service industry, the menu Doris created at Zeppoli's features both traditional Italian foods and innovative dishes using favorite Italian ingredients. Fresh homemade pasta, ravioli, bread, soups, and sauces are available for takeout. Zeppoli's also offers catering services.

**Cook's Note:**
Don't want to worry about the bread bowl? No problem. This dip can be baked in a round, glass baking dish sprayed with cooking spray.

# Zeppoli's
# Garlic Butter

*This compound butter is great for garlic bread, mussels, fish, shrimp scampi, and pasta, and for cooking steaks. It can be stored in the refrigerator in an airtight container for two weeks or can be frozen.*

1 pound butter, softened
1 tablespoon dried parsley
1 teaspoon dried chives
1 teaspoon dried basil
6 cloves garlic, minced

Combine all ingredients in a large bowl.

What is a zeppoli? Zeppole, the correct Italian term, are small balls of fried dough, topped with powdered sugar, similar in taste to what we call funnel cakes in Virginia. They are traditional desserts of Southeast Italy, often served at festivals, street fairs, and on religious holidays such as the Feast of St. Joseph, celebrated on March 19. On that day, Zeppoli's offers free zeppole to its customers.

# Café de Bangkok's
# Chicken Satay and Peanut Sauce

*Though it was not around when we were in school, current students strongly encouraged us to dine at this super-popular, family-owned, Thai restaurant. Given our obsession with peanut butter, we were thrilled to have this recipe.*

Serves 2

1 (13.5-ounce) can coconut milk
1 teaspoon grated fresh ginger
2 tablespoons curry powder
2 tablespoons fish sauce
1 pound skinless, boneless chicken breasts, cut into strips
20 bamboo skewers, soaked in water 30 minutes
coconut oil, for grilling

Whisk together the coconut milk, ginger, curry powder, and fish sauce in a large mixing bowl. Add chicken strips into the mixture and toss until well coated. Cover with plastic wrap and let the chicken marinate in the refrigerator for at least 2 hours.

Place chicken strips on bamboo skewers. Place a grill pan over medium heat and brush it with coconut oil to prevent chicken from sticking. Grill the chicken until nicely seared and cooked through. Serve on a platter with peanut sauce on the side.

### For peanut sauce:
1 (13.5-ounce) can coconut milk
1 cup sugar
2 tablespoons red curry paste*
2 tablespoons tamarind concentrate (see Cook's Note below)
2 tablespoons soy sauce or fish sauce
¼ cup natural creamy peanut butter
¼ cup warm water
¼ cup crushed peanuts, for garnish

Place all ingredients into a medium saucepan and bring to a boil, whisking constantly. Let the mixture simmer 5–10 minutes over low heat. Be careful not to let the mixture scorch at the bottom of the pot. Remove from heat and pour the sauce into a serving bowl. Garnish with crushed peanuts.

*Substitute Thai red chili powder if you prefer a spicier peanut sauce.

**Cook's Note:** If you have difficulty finding tamarind paste, you can replace it with ⅓ cup of lime juice mixed with ⅓ cup of water.

# Deet's Place
## Sundried Tomato Dip

*This dip (and the awesome bagel chips) served as a late-night meal for me during freshman year. Anytime I was hit by homesickness, or stress from studying for a big test, you could find me at Deet's with this dip and a large chai latte (okay, fine, and maybe an ice cream too).*

*—Kris*

1 (8-ounce) package cream cheese, slightly softened
2 tablespoons chopped sun-dried tomatoes
1 tablespoon chopped onion
⅛ teaspoon salt
⅛ teaspoon pepper
bagel chips or pita crisps for dipping

Place cream cheese, sun-dried tomatoes, onion, salt, and pepper in a food processor. Pulse until the dip is creamy and smooth.

Keep in an airtight container in the refrigerator until ready to serve.

# Soups, Salads, Sandwiches

◆ ◆ ◆

West End Market's Lobster Bisque
West End Market's Chipotle Tortilla Soup
West End Market's Spicy Asian Chicken Wrap
West End Market's Cutting Edge Deli's Hokie Club
West End Market's Broccoli Cheese Soup
A Homage to Boudreaux's Shrimp Po' Boy
Lefty's Ham and Asparagus Sandwich
Gourmet Pantry's Lentil Salad
Norrine and Ed Spencer's Alfredo Mushroom Soup
Big Al's Chicken Noodle Soup
Preston's Spring Minestrone Soup

*West End Market's*
*Hokie Club*
*Pg. 52*

# West End Market's
## Lobster Bisque

*Is this recipe labor intensive? Yes. Is it worth it? Absolutely. Not to say that students don't appreciate the work that goes into West End's creations, but testing this recipe gave us even greater admiration for the amount of detail it takes for the chefs of West End to produce delicious results.*

Serves 8–10

**For the stock:**
4 tablespoons unsalted butter
2 lobsters, cooked and removed from shell (do not discard shell)
2 cups chopped yellow onion
2 cups chopped celery
1 tablespoon minced garlic
1 tablespoon paprika
2 tablespoons tomato paste
½ cup brandy
1½ teaspoons whole black peppercorns
½ teaspoon dried thyme
2 bay leaves
2 quarts water

Melt the butter in a stockpot on medium-high heat. Add the lobster shells and cook for about 3–5 minutes. Add the onion, celery, garlic, and paprika, and cook for 5–10 more minutes, or until vegetables are soft. Stir in the tomato paste and cook for 3–5 minutes. Stir in Brandy to deglaze the pan and cook until all the liquid is absorbed. Add peppercorns, thyme, bay leaves and water. Bring to a boil. Reduce heat to low and simmer uncovered for 45 minutes. Strain into a clean, empty stockpot.

**For the roux:**
¾ cup flour
6 tablespoons unsalted butter

Melt butter in a heavy skillet on medium-high heat. When the foaming subsides, quickly stir in the flour using a wire whisk. Reduce heat to medium. Continue to whisk until the roux turns light yellow. Transfer mixture to a small, clean mixing bowl and let cool to room temperature.

**For the soup:**
2½ cups heavy cream
¾ pound lobster claw and knuckle meat
½ teaspoon salt
¼ teaspoon crab seasoning
¾ teaspoon hot sauce
½ teaspoon Worcestershire sauce
2½ ounces sherry

Place the stockpot of strained stock on medium heat. Add the roux and whisk until combined. Lower heat and add heavy cream, lobster meat, and seasonings. Simmer for 10 minutes. Whisk in the sherry and serve hot.

**Chef's Tip:**
A roux is a combination of fat and starch that, when blended together and added to a liquid, aids in thickening the liquid. The standard rule for combining roux and stock for velouté is to add hot roux to cold stock or cold roux to hot stock. This will help to avoid lumps.

## West End Market's
# Chipotle Tortilla Soup

*This is one of Chef Bratton's favorite dishes, and after making it at home, we know why: it is comfort food at its best. Serve with Pico de Gallo (recipe follows).*

Serves 12

1 tablespoon olive oil
1 medium yellow onion, chopped (about 1 cup)
1½ tablespoons minced garlic
1½ tablespoons chipotle peppers
2½ teaspoons chili powder
½ teaspoon ground cumin
2 quarts plus 2¾ cups water
3 tablespoons plus 2¼ teaspoons chicken bouillon
¾ cup canned diced tomatoes
¾ cup tomato puree
½ pound organic yellow corn tortilla chips
1¼ teaspoon finely chopped cilantro
1 pound smoked or roasted chicken breast, cubed
¼ teaspoon Kosher salt
2¾ teaspoons lime juice

Warm the olive oil in a large stockpot on medium heat. Add the onions and cook until translucent, about 3 minutes. Add the garlic and continue to cook for 1 minute. Add the chipotle peppers, chili powder, and cumin, and cook for 5 more minutes. Add the water, bouillon, tomatoes, tomato puree, and tortilla chips, and bring to a boil. Reduce heat and simmer uncovered for 30 minutes. Remove from heat. Puree until thick and creamy with an immersion blender. Stir in cilantro, chicken, salt, and lime juice. Garnish with pico de gallo and sour cream.

**Chef's Tip:**
**If you do not have an immersion blender, you may ladle the soup into a blender or food processor and puree until thick and creamy. Pour soup back into stockpot and serve warm.**

# Pico de Gallo

1 cup small diced tomatoes
1 cup small diced red peppers
1 cup small diced green peppers
1 jalapeño pepper, seeded and minced
¼ cup finely chopped red onion
2 teaspoons finely chopped cilantro
1¾ teaspoons fresh lime juice
½ teaspoon Kosher salt

Toss together all ingredients in a small bowl. Keep refrigerated.

# West End Market's
# Spicy Asian Chicken Wrap

*This recipe came about as a suggestion from a former manager at West End and has been a huge hit ever since. West End prepares these wraps with its house teriyaki sauce (recipe follows). Chef Bratton ensures that it takes no longer than 45 seconds to build each wrap to keep the traffic at West End moving. Impressive.*

Serves 6

2 pounds breaded chicken tenders*
1½ tablespoons olive oil
4 ounces sliced onions (about ½ cup)
4 ounces sliced red peppers (about ½ cup)
4 ounces sliced green peppers (about ½ cup)
12 ounces teriyaki sauce, heated—store bought or homemade
6 (12-inch) flour tortillas
6 leaves green lettuce
1 cup jasmine rice, cooked
1¼ ounces packaged fried wonton strips

Preheat oven to 450°F.

Place the chicken tenders on a foil lined sheet pan and bake in oven for 10 minutes.

Warm olive oil in a large sauté pan over medium-high heat. Add the onions and peppers, and sauté until they are just tender, about 5 minutes. Remove from heat.

Place the chicken tenders in a bowl along with the hot teriyaki sauce, and gently toss to coat.

**To assemble:**
Lay one tortilla on a flat surface. Place a piece of lettuce in the center of the tortilla. Next, place a spoonful of rice on top of the lettuce. Place two of the chicken tenders over the rice and then top with some of the cooked peppers and onions. Finish with some fried wonton strips. Fold both sides of the tortilla about 1 inch to the center. Pull one end over the filling while holding the sides and roll up into a burrito shape. Repeat with remaining tortillas.

*We used store-bought breaded chicken for testing purposes.

# Teriyaki Sauce

¼ cup soy sauce
½ cup sugar
1½ teaspoons minced ginger
2¼ teaspoons minced garlic
1 cup water
1 tablespoon pineapple juice
1 tablespoon plus 1 teaspoon chili paste
1 tablespoon rice wine
1 tablespoon plus ¾ teaspoon cornstarch
1½ teaspoon sesame seeds, toasted

Combine the soy sauce, sugar, ginger, garlic, water, pineapple juice, and chili paste in a medium saucepan on medium-low heat. Bring to a simmer.

Stir together the rice wine and cornstarch in a small bowl until combined. Whisk this into the soy mixture. Bring back to a simmer and add the sesame seeds. Continue to cook until sauce forms a syrupy glaze, about 4 minutes.

# West End Market's
# Cutting Edge Deli's Hokie Club

*This is West End's most popular sandwich. Choose the best deli meat you can afford and look for thick potato bread.*

Serves 1

3 slices potato bread
2¼ teaspoons mayonnaise
1 slice roasted turkey breast
2 slices cooked bacon
2 slices Swiss cheese
2 leaves green lettuce
2 slices tomato, about 1/8-inch thick
1 slice roast beef
1 slice ham
1 slice American cheese

Toast bread slices and assemble as follows:

Spread bottom piece of bread with half of the mayonnaise and top with turkey, bacon, Swiss cheese, and one each of lettuce and tomato.

Spread middle piece with the remaining mayonnaise and top with roast beef, ham, American cheese, and one slice each of lettuce and tomato.

Top with remaining slice of bread.

# Broccoli Cheese Soup

*This soup is therapy in a bowl. It is a go-to for rainy days, poor grades, and breakups. Spoon optional.*

Serves 6–8

**For the roux:**
¾ cup flour
6 tablespoons unsalted butter

Melt butter in a medium skillet on medium-high heat. When the foaming subsides, stir in the flour using a whisk and reduce heat to medium. Continue to stir until the roux turns light yellow. Transfer immediately to a clean bowl and set aside until ready to use.

**For the soup:**
4 tablespoons unsalted butter
1 cup diced yellow onion
½ cup diced celery
1 pound fresh broccoli, washed and chopped into ¼-inch pieces
3 ounces fresh shredded carrots (about 1 large carrot)
1 tablespoon plus ½ teaspoon Kosher salt
1 quart plus 3 cups milk
1½ cups heavy cream
12 ounces shredded cheddar cheese

Melt butter in a large stockpot over medium heat. Add the onion and celery and cook until tender, about 10 minutes. Add the broccoli, carrots, and salt, and continue to cook until the broccoli is slightly tender, about 10 minutes.

Add the roux and continue to cook for 3 minutes, stirring frequently. Add both the milk and cream, and bring to a simmer, stirring frequently. Simmer for 15–20 minutes. Add the cheese and stir until melted. Serve hot.

If you don't own a deep fry thermometer, the best way to check the readiness of the oil is to drop in a small piece of bread. If the bread sizzles and stays afloat, the oil is ready. If the bread turns color too quickly, the oil is too hot; reduce the temperature.

# A Homage to Boudreaux's
## Shrimp Po' Boy

*This recipe is inspired by the po' boy at Boudreaux's, a long standing restaurant on Main Street. In fact, Boudreaux's was the first restaurant to offer full food service, meaning made-to-order from scratch. The rooftop deck is a huge draw and its authentic Creole cuisine is seriously good.*

Serves 4

vegetable oil
1 cup flour
1 cup cornmeal
2 tablespoons Cajun seasoning
½ teaspoon cayenne pepper
1 teaspoon salt
1 cup buttermilk
1 teaspoon hot sauce
16–20 shrimp, peeled and deveined
4 hoagie rolls
remoulade sauce, store bought
4 leaves romaine lettuce
2 tomatoes, sliced

Whisk together flour, cornmeal, Cajun seasoning, and ½ teaspoon salt in a large mixing bowl. Set aside. Whisk together buttermilk and hot sauce in a separate medium bowl.

Lay shrimp flat on paper towels and season with ½ teaspoon salt.

Add enough vegetable oil to a medium saucepan to reach a depth of 1½ inches. Place on medium-high heat until oil is approximately 365°F.

Meanwhile, dip each piece of shrimp in the buttermilk mixture, dredge in the flour mixture, and place on a large plate. Repeat with remaining shrimp.

Carefully place no more than 5 pieces of shrimp in the hot oil. Do not overcrowd, or the temperature of the oil will drop and the shrimp will not fry properly. Cook until golden brown, approximately 2 minutes. Remove shrimp with a slotted spoon and place on a clean plate lined with a paper towel. Repeat with remaining shrimp.

Slice hoagie rolls and toast until lightly golden. Spread both sides with remoulade and place romaine leaves, followed by 2–3 tomato slices, finished with 4–5 pieces of shrimp on each roll.

# Lefty's
# Ham and Asparagus Sandwich

*Our waitress persuaded us to try this sandwich as it's one of Lefty's most popular lunch items. Thick slices of ham are grilled and paired with bite-sized pieces of steamed asparagus and placed on a roll that gets a subtle "kick" from herbed goat cheese. Lefty's serves their sandwiches with house-made potato chips, which we're pretty sure can't be found anywhere else in Blacksburg.*

Serves 6

**For the herbed goat cheese:**
2 cups cream cheese
1 cup goat cheese
1 cup Parmesan cheese
4 small cloves garlic, roughly chopped
½ teaspoon salt
½ teaspoon pepper
1 tablespoon dried basil
1 tablespoon dried thyme
1 tablespoon dried rosemary
3 tablespoons half and half

Place all ingredients, except for the half and half, in a food processor and pulse several times until the mixture is thick and combined. Add in half and half and pulse again until it is spreadable. If the spread is too thick for your liking, add in more half and half, a tablespoon at a time until desired consistency.

6 hoagie rolls, toasted
¼ cup chopped walnuts
12 cooked asparagus spears, chopped
4½ ounces thick sliced ham, warmed on grill or skillet
12 tomato slices

Spread herbed goat cheese on toasted rolls. Add chopped walnuts and asparagus on top of the cheese so they stay in place. Place ham on top of the walnuts and asparagus. Top with two tomato slices per sandwich.

# Gourmet Pantry's
# Lentil Salad

*Owner Roya Gharavi will show you how to enhance your cooking skills regardless of your existing culinary knowledge. You'll learn how to cook healthy foods with ingredients that are fresh and accessible. Check out gourmetpantryonline.com for the current cooking class schedule.*

Serves 4-6

1½ cups French green lentils, rinsed and picked over
3½ cups water
1 cup chopped onion
1 or 2 sprigs fresh thyme
1 bay leaf
½ teaspoon salt
pinch of ground cloves or 3 pieces whole cloves (optional)

Place lentils, water, chopped onion, thyme, bay leaf, salt, and ground cloves (if using) into a medium saucepan. Bring to a boil, cover, and reduce the heat to a simmer. Simmer for about 25–30 minutes; lentils should retain their shape but be cooked through. Remove from heat and cool until lukewarm. Drain any remaining liquid. Pour lentils into a mixing bowl and discard herbs.

**For the dressing:**
2 or 3 tablespoons white wine vinegar, plus more to taste
4 tablespoons extra-virgin olive oil, plus more to taste
½ teaspoon salt, plus more to taste
¼ teaspoon freshly ground pepper, plus more to taste
1 tablespoon Dijon mustard
hot sauce, to taste

Combine all and mix well.

**To assemble:**
1 large tomato, chopped into ½-inch pieces (about 1¼ cup)
1 small green pepper, chopped
1 cup marinated artichoke hearts (from a jar), chopped
⅓ cup finely chopped shallots
2 cloves garlic, minced
2 tablespoons slivered, toasted almonds

Whisk together vinegar, olive oil, salt, pepper, Dijon mustard, and hot sauce in a small bowl.

Add tomato, green pepper, artichoke, shallots, and garlic to the bowl with the lentils. Pour the dressing over and fold in gently. Taste and adjust the seasoning. Sprinkle with slivered almonds before serving.

# Norrine and Ed Spencer's
# Alfredo Mushroom Soup

*As a resident advisor and a student in the Pamplin College of Business, I had the great pleasure of knowing both Dr. Edward Spencer and Dr. Norrine Bailey Spencer (1947-2009). The Spencer's served Virginia Tech with honor and made countless contributions in the community. Here's one of Ed's personal favorites, a delicious mushroom soup that Norrine would often make.*

*- Naren Aryal*
*1992 Virginia Tech (B.S. Finance)*

Serves 4

¼ cup olive oil
¼ cup unsalted butter
1 clove garlic, crushed
1 medium white or yellow onion, finely chopped (about 1 cup)
1 (6-ounce) can tomato paste
1 pound mushrooms, sliced
¼ cup white wine
3 cups chicken broth
3 egg yolks
½ cup Parmesan cheese
¼ cup finely chopped parsley
salt and pepper, to taste
croutons or garlic bread, for serving

Heat olive oil and butter in a large stockpot on medium heat. Add garlic and onion, and cook until onions are translucent, about 5 minutes. Add tomato paste. Add mushrooms, wine, and chicken stock. Season to taste with salt and pepper. Bring to a boil, lower the heat, and simmer for 10–15 minutes. Remove from heat.

Whisk together egg yolks, Parmesan, and parsley in a small bowl. Add one ladle of hot soup from the pot to the egg mixture and whisk quickly. Pour mixture into the stockpot. Be careful to not let the soup boil at this point. Stir another minute. Serve immediately with croutons or garlic bread.

# Big Al's
# Chicken Noodle Soup

*We've heard people travel far distances for this soup, so we had to try it for ourselves. It is best served with a grilled cheese on Texas toast. Now, if only this soup could cook itself when you're sick.*

Serves 6–8

6–8 boneless chicken thighs
5 chicken bouillon cubes
½ cup diced carrots
¼ cup chopped celery
¼ teaspoon black pepper
¼ teaspoon poultry seasoning
4 ounces wide egg noodles

Place chicken in a large stockpot and barely cover with water. Bring water to a boil and cook until tender, about 10 minutes. Remove chicken from stockpot with tongs and place on a clean cutting board. Reserve remaining liquid and set aside. Chop chicken into bite-sized pieces.

Add 3 quarts of water and bouillon cubes to the stockpot with the chicken broth. Add carrots, celery, pepper, and poultry seasoning. Bring mixture to a boil and add cooked chicken and egg noodles. Stir and simmer for 8–10 minutes or until pasta is cooked and vegetables are tender. Season to taste with salt and pepper.

You might be surprised to know that Big Al's actually started out as a hair salon named Big Al's Looking Glass, and since 1977 this family-owned business has been transformed into a household name in Blacksburg.

The Edwards family consists of Big Al himself, matriarch Shirl, daughter Julie, and son Billy. Entry into the food business came by way of Big Al's Hotdogs, which was in the same location but limited to a 10 x 10-foot space downstairs. According to Shirl, it was Billy who inspired the family to open a restaurant and bar, and so the family hired close friend Jimmy Dobbins as head chef and Big Al's was opened in 1998.

The family held a legendary launch party and the restaurant's popularity skyrocketed. In 2000 the hair salon closed and the family opened Poor Billy's, a fine dining establishment highly regarded for its seafood and sushi. In 2012 the business further expanded by launching Poor Billy's Small Plates in a separate dining spot located just behind the building that houses the other restaurants.

There are two items of decor that must be noted: a banner of the 1999 perfect season signed by the entire football team as well as the goal post (hung on the ceiling) that students removed from the field after winning against Boston College that same year.

It's no wonder that students (and even alumni) have a special allegiance to the Big Al's brand. The Edwards made us feel like family when we met them, graciously greeting us with a hug and a piping hot bowl of chicken noodle soup.

We asked Shirl when she knew her business was a success and she told us that she was wearing a Big Al sweatshirt at an airport across the country when someone approached her and said, "I went to Big Al's all the time when I was in school." It must be neat for the Edwards family to realize that a business they built for their livelihood is now an institution.

# Preston's
# Spring Minestrone Soup

*This recipe comes from Preston's Chef Jason Smith, located at the Inn of Virginia Tech. The staff at the hotel raves about his culinary skills. When we cooked this ourselves, it made the house smell delicious and we had plenty for leftovers, and then some. Serve alongside a fresh salad for a fantastic and healthy meal.*

Serves 6–8

4 cups vegetable broth
1 (28-ounce) can diced tomatoes
4 cloves garlic, finely chopped
2 pounds fingerling potatoes, cut into ¾-inch pieces
1 pound artichoke hearts (canned), roughly chopped
3¾ cups cooked chickpeas
4 tablespoons extra-virgin olive oil
12 green onions, finely chopped
2 cups green peas
1 pound asparagus, cut into ¾-inch pieces
salt and pepper, to taste
basil pesto and shaved pecorino Romano cheese, for topping

Add the vegetable broth, diced tomatoes, garlic, and fingerling potatoes to a large stockpot. Bring to a boil, lower the heat and let simmer for 15 minutes.

Add the artichoke hearts and chickpeas; let simmer for an additional 10 minutes. Lastly, add the olive oil, green onions, green peas, and asparagus. Cook for 15 minutes on medium heat.

Add salt and pepper to taste. Ladle into bowls and garnish with pesto and cheese.

# Main Dishes

West End Market's Grilled Old Hickory Burger

West End Market's Marinara Sauce

A Homage to Boudreaux's Jambalaya

West End Market's Cajun Cream Pasta Sauce

Cabo Fish Taco's Soy Ginger Shrimp Taco

West End Market's London Broil with Mushroom Sauce

Gourmet Pantry's Lemon Pepper Shrimp with Pasta

Gourmet Pantry's Chicken with Roasted Red Chili Paste and Fresh Basil

622 North's Corn Encrusted Tilapia

Pita Vera's Chicken Kabob

Ellen Stewart's Farmers' Market Harvest Pork Skillet

Top of the Stairs' Ribs

Our Daily Bread's Beef Bourguignonne

Our Daily Bread's Quiche Lorraine

SAL's Seafood Pescatore

SAL's Chicken Bruschetta Pizza Pop

Castle's Kettle and Pub's Irish Coddle

Big Al's Meatloaf

*Cabo Fish Taco's Soy
Ginger Shrimp Taco
Pg. 76*

# West End Market's
# Grilled Old Hickory Burger

*This is Krista's husband's—and probably every other frat boy's—favorite dish. He still orders this every time he visits Blacksburg.*

Serves 6

2 pounds ground beef chuck, formed into 6 patties
2 tablespoons steak seasoning
6 slices ham
6 Kaiser rolls, sliced in half
2 tablespoons unsalted butter, melted
6 slices American cheese
12 slices bacon, cooked
¾ cup barbeque sauce
6 leaves green lettuce
1 large tomato, sliced 1/8 - inch thick
3 ounces sliced red onion
4½ ounces dill pickle chips

Preheat broiler and preheat grill or grill pan.

Season both sides of hamburger patties with the steak seasoning. Cook hamburgers to an internal temperature of 155°F. Place the ham slices on the grill and cook for a couple minutes on both sides. Meanwhile, brush the inside of the buns with the melted butter and toast under the broiler until golden brown.

### To assemble:
Place a slice of cheese on each burger, then a grilled ham slice. Top with the bacon and transfer to the bottom half of the Kaiser roll. Spoon a couple tablespoons of the barbeque sauce over each burger. Place the lettuce, tomato, onion, and pickle chips over the sauce and finish by covering with the top toasted roll.

# West End Market's
# Marinara Sauce

*This dish alone is the reason why Krista had the endurance to survive HighTech training. You laugh, but that training consisted of sprinting the steps of the stadium, max testing in the weight room, and 3-hour practices. Some serious carbohydrates were needed for all of that. This sauce gets a huge help from the red wine. Use a wine that you would want to drink. Believe us, it makes a difference.*

2 tablespoons unsalted butter
2 tablespoons olive oil
1 medium white onion, chopped (about 1 cup)
2 tablespoons minced garlic
¾ cup red wine
1 (28-ounce) can diced tomatoes
1 cup tomato puree
1 cup tomato juice
1 tablespoon chopped fresh basil
1 teaspoon chopped fresh oregano
1 tablespoon brown sugar
1½ teaspoons salt
½ teaspoon cracked black pepper

Warm the butter and olive oil in a large saucepan on medium-low heat. Add the onions and garlic, and sauté until they are tender, about 3–5 minutes. Add the red wine and cook until all the liquid has been absorbed. Add the tomatoes, tomato puree, tomato juice, basil, oregano, brown sugar, salt, and pepper, and simmer for 30 minutes. Serve over hot pasta.

**Chef's Tip:**
**Use good quality tomatoes, such as Muir Glen or San Marzano.**

# A Homage to Boudreaux's
## Jambalaya

*We created this recipe as a homage to Boudreaux's, one of our favorite restaurants in Blacksburg. Be prepared to make this recipe several times—Kris made it three times in two days for her husband—not because you'll screw it up but because the leftovers will disappear out of your fridge faster than you can say, "Bourbon Street."*

Serves 2–4

4 tablespoons olive oil
4 ounces chicken breasts, cubed
12 medium uncooked shrimp, peeled, deveined, and chopped
5 ounces Andouille sausage, sliced
¼ cup chopped yellow onion
¼ cup chopped green bell pepper
¼ cup chopped red bell pepper
2 tablespoons minced garlic
½ cup chopped tomatoes
3 bay leaves
1 tablespoon Cajun seasoning
1 teaspoon Worcestershire sauce
¾ cup uncooked white rice
3 cups chicken broth
salt and pepper, to taste
chopped fresh parsley, for garnish

Heat 2 tablespoons olive oil in a large stockpot or Dutch oven on medium heat. First, cook the chicken until browned on all sides, about 5 minutes. Remove and place in clean bowl. Next, sear the shrimp, about 2–3 minutes. Remove and place in bowl with chicken. Finally, brown the sausage, about 4 minutes. Remove and place in the same bowl.

Heat remaining 2 tablespoons olive oil in the same stockpot over medium-high heat. Add the onion, green pepper, and red pepper, and sauté for 3 minutes. Add garlic, tomatoes, bay leaves, Cajun seasoning, and Worcestershire sauce.

Stir in the rice and slowly add broth. Reduce heat to medium and cook until rice absorbs liquid and becomes tender, stirring occasionally, about 15 minutes.

When rice is just tender, add shrimp, chicken, and sausage to the pot. Cook until meat is completely done, about 10 minutes more. Add salt, pepper, and Cajun seasoning to taste. Garnish with parsley.

# West End Market's
# Cajun Cream Pasta Sauce

*This sauce is Alfredo in high gear, a one-handed touchdown pass caught in the last few minutes of a football game, a ... okay, you get our point. When we made this sauce, we were overcome by the amazing aroma that filled the room. It is abundantly flavorful and blissfully silky. Not convinced how crazy we are for this dish? One of us had her head buried in the stockpot for constant inhalation; the other declared that she wanted to pour it on her face. Don't be intimidated by the long list of ingredients. Most of them literally get tossed in the pot at the same time and do the work for you.*

Serves 8–10

¼ cup chopped shallots
¼ cup diced celery
¾ cup diced green pepper
¾ cup diced red pepper
3 tablespoons minced garlic
¼ teaspoon dried oregano
⅛ teaspoon ground cayenne pepper
¼ teaspoon dried basil
⅛ teaspoon dried thyme
1 tablespoon Cajun seasoning
1 teaspoon ground black pepper
2 cups white wine
3 teaspoons chicken bouillon
3 cups water
¼ cup cornstarch
¼ cup white wine
3 cups heavy cream
12 ounces grated Parmesan cheese

Combine the first 14 ingredients in a large stockpot over medium-high heat. Bring to a boil and lower the heat to low and simmer. Continue to simmer and reduce the volume to two-thirds.

Combine the cornstarch with the second amount of wine. Add the cornstarch mixture to the stockpot and stir continuously to thicken the soup. Once thickened, stir in the cream and cheese until combined. Using an immersion blender or a food processor, puree the sauce until creamy. Serve with hot pasta.

Cabo Fish Taco's
# Soy Ginger
# Shrimp Taco

One word: *ridiculous!* The deep fried shrimp are crunchy, tangy, and presented beautifully with a speckling of sesame seeds. No wonder current students told us we needed to immediately order this dish. It is exactly as they've described: addictive.

Serves 4–6

vegetable oil, for frying
1½ pounds uncooked shrimp, peeled and deveined
1 cup flour
1 cup dark beer
1 cup sugar
⅓ cup soy sauce
¼ cup white distilled vinegar
4 tablespoons peeled and minced fresh ginger
12 flour tortillas
2 medium tomatoes, diced
3 cups shredded cabbage
1 or 2 avocados, thinly sliced
2 cups cheddar-jack cheese
scallions and sesame seeds, for garnish

---

Pour vegetable oil into a heavy, medium saucepan to a depth of 1½ inches. Set aside.

Lay shrimp out on a paper towel and blot dry.

Whisk together flour and beer in a large bowl until combined.

Combine sugar, soy sauce, vinegar, and sherry in a medium saucepan over low heat. Cook until sugar is dissolved, about 5 minutes. Increase heat to medium until liquid begins to foam and rise, about 3 minutes. Stir frequently. Continue to cook until volume is reduced by one half, about 20–25 minutes. You may need to reduce the heat if it is cooking too quickly. The glaze should appear thick and syrupy. While it is cooking, you will begin to cook the shrimp.

Meanwhile, heat the vegetable oil on medium-high heat until a thermometer registers 350°F. Place all of the shrimp in the beer batter and toss until well coated. Cover two plates with paper towels and set out a large slotted spoon. With another large spoon, test one piece of shrimp first, by placing it carefully in the hot oil. If it darkens quickly, you'll need to lower the heat. If the shrimp sinks or isn't bubbling rapidly, increase the heat. Cook the shrimp about 60–90 seconds, until deep golden brown. Fry 6–7 shrimp at a time, taking care not to overcrowd or the temperature of the oil will drop and the shrimp will not cook properly. Remove shrimp from the oil with a slotted spoon and place on the plates covered with paper towels.

Toss the shrimp carefully with the glaze on a clean baking sheet or in a large bowl.

Pour vegetable oil in a large skillet to a depth of ½-inch and heat on medium-high until temperature reaches 350°F. Fry tortillas one at a time on both sides for 15 seconds. Hang shells vertically to drip dry. Do not lay them flat on top of each other or they will become saturated with oil.

On each tortilla, in this order, spread some avocado, sprinkle cheese, add shredded cabbage and then diced tomatoes. Add fried shrimp and garnish with sesame seeds and scallions.

The menu at Cabo Fish Taco reads, "This menu was created by friends who agree that great food begins with the freshest ingredients." If you dine at this relatively new, breezy hot spot on Main Street, you will sense its mission immediately.

Cabo has the most diverse selection of tequila in the state of Virginia (72 different brands) along with thirteen twists on the classic margarita. Cabo is the place to go when you want a slice of summer. Its location in Charlotte, North Carolina, is so popular that it has been featured on the Food Network's *Diners, Drive-in's, and Dives.*

We tried our best to obtain the house-made margarita recipe, but the staff holds it sacred. After trying the Perfect Wave margarita, we understood. It was fresh, not at all sugary and straight-up loco. Between the inventive menu, the sultry flavors, and the cool atmosphere, we'll use a line directly from part-owner Gary and say that Cabo Fish Taco is "Right On."

Chef's Tip:
A "slurry" is a thickening agent which is made by combining a starch and a liquid. This technique will help produce a thick and smooth product without creating any lumps.

West End Market's

# London Broil with Mushroom Sauce

*This is, by far, the most popular dish at West End Market and probably at Virginia Tech. It is typically served with its ultra creamy counterpart, garlic whipped potatoes (see page 110 for recipe). West End's London broil is consumed by approximately 750 students per day and now, by you. Choice flank steak is penetrated with an Asian-style marinade that both tenderizes and flavors the meat, which will crackle as it's pulled off the grill. Let it rest before carving so the juices redistribute and keep the dish moist. Top with the tangy mushroom sauce.*

Serves 2–4

2¼ pounds choice flank steak
¼ cup plus ½ teaspoon teriyaki sauce
1½ tablespoons red wine vinegar
1½ tablespoons soy sauce
1½ tablespoons Worcestershire sauce
¼ cup minced yellow onion
1 clove garlic, minced
2 bay leaves
pinch ground cloves
2 tablespoons white wine
vegetable oil, for grilling

Place the steak in a large ziplock bag. Combine all ingredients in a bowl and whisk together to blend. Carefully pour the marinade into the bag with the meat. Seal the bag, place into a large baking dish, and marinate in the refrigerator 3–4 hours.

Preheat grill or grill pan on medium-high heat. Brush the grill with vegetable oil. Remove the steak from the marinade and cook to desired doneness. For medium rare, cook about 6–8 minutes per side. Remove from heat and allow meat to rest for 5 minutes prior to slicing. Using a sharp knife, cut across the grain of the meat thinly. Serve with the mushroom sauce.

### *For the mushroom sauce:*
6 ounces sliced mushrooms
2½ teaspoons sherry
2½ teaspoons red wine vinegar
3 tablespoons plus ¾ teaspoon soy sauce
3 tablespoons plus ¾ teaspoon Worcestershire sauce
2¼ cups water
2 teaspoons minced garlic
dash ground cloves
½ cup plus 1 tablespoon and 2 teaspoons teriyaki sauce
¼ cup cornstarch
3 tablespoons water

Place the first 9 ingredients in a 2-quart saucepan. Bring to a boil, reduce heat to a simmer, and cook for about 5 minutes. Combine cornstarch with water in a small bowl to make a slurry (see Chef's Tip). Drizzle the slurry slowly into the simmering liquid to thicken. Bring back to a simmer. Remove from the heat and serve.

# Gourmet Pantry's
# Lemon Pepper Shrimp with Pasta

*Owner Roya Gharavi teaches her students that it is not difficult to cook fast and healthy dishes; this recipe is a great example of that. The ingredients are accessible and the result is a deeply satisfying meal.*

Serves 4–6

1 pound pasta, any kind
2 tablespoons olive oil
1 pound uncooked shrimp, peeled, deveined, and blotted dry
1 shallot, diced
3 cloves garlic, minced
½ cup white wine
½ cup low-sodium chicken broth
juice of 2 lemons
freshly ground pepper and salt
2 tablespoons chopped fresh parsley

Cook pasta according to package directions.

Heat 1 tablespoon olive oil in a large skillet on medium-high heat. Sear shrimp for approximately 1 minute on one side and 30 seconds on the other side. With a slotted spoon, remove shrimp and place on a clean plate.

Add 1 tablespoon olive oil to the same skillet and place on medium-low heat. Add diced shallot and sauté until tender, approximately 2–3 minutes. Add garlic and sauté for 30 seconds.

Add wine, chicken broth, and lemon juice. Bring to a boil and immediately remove skillet from heat. Add generous amounts of pepper and salt. Finish with parsley.

Serve pasta on a plate, arrange shrimp on top, and ladle sauce over top.

Gourmet Pantry's

# Chicken with Roasted Chili Paste and Fresh Basil

*This is another simple one-pot dinner brought to you by Roya Gharavi. We tested this recipe using Thai basil, but you can also use regular Italian basil and achieve equally tasty results.*

Serves 4

3 tablespoons vegetable oil
1 tablespoon chopped garlic
1 pound chicken breasts, cubed
3 tablespoons roasted chili paste
2 tablespoons fish sauce
¼ cup water or chicken broth
1 teaspoon sugar
1 cup Asian or Italian basil leaves
1 red bell pepper, cut into long thin strips

Heat oil in a large, deep skillet or a wok over medium-high heat until a bit of garlic sizzles. Add the garlic and toss well until fragrant, about 1 minute. Add the chicken and toss.

Add the roasted chili paste, fish sauce, water, and sugar and continue cooking and tossing occasionally until the chicken is cooked through, and is coated with sauce, about 5–7 minutes.

Add the basil leaves and toss well. Turn onto a serving platter, garnish with red pepper strips and serve hot.

622 NORTH

# 622 North's
# Corn Encrusted Tilapia

*We love the decor almost as much as the menu at 622 North, from the gorgeous wall color down to the window treatments. But what really makes this upscale restaurant provocative are the ultramodern chalkboards marked with the daily specials: soups, fish, and most importantly, martinis. This is another excellent recipe by 622 North's head chef, Tom Newton. 622 North is owned by Frank Perkovich, a transplant from California, who shares our admiration for Tom's creations.*

Serves 4

4 (8-ounce) tilapia filets
salt and pepper, to taste
4 eggs
1 cup flour
vegetable oil, for frying
1 pound corn kernels (frozen, canned, or fresh)
2 tablespoons olive oil
4 small shallots, thinly sliced
½ cup dry white wine
1 cup beef or veal stock
4 tablespoons unsalted butter, cubed

Season fish with salt and pepper. Beat eggs in a small bowl. Put flour in a small bowl or dish.

Pour enough oil to coat the bottom of a large skillet and place on medium-high heat. Dip fish into eggs and dredge in flour. Reserve left-over flour. Working one at a time, hold fish filet flat in your palm (slightly cupped) and cover evenly with ¼ of the corn. Quickly invert fish, corn-side down, into pan. Repeat with all fish, working in batches with fresh oil if skillet is not large enough. Cook fish on corn side for 5–6 minutes until opaque almost all the way through and egg has cooked. Gently slide a thin spatula underneath and flip fish. Corn should be nicely browned and bound to fish. Cook for an additional 2–3 minutes.

Meanwhile, sauté shallots in olive oil in a small saucepan on medium heat for 2–3 minutes, until lightly caramelized. Deglaze the pan with white wine and let reduce by 90 percent. Add beef stock and bring to steady simmer. Roll tablespoons of butter in remaining flour and add to sauce. Remove pan from heat and stir quickly until sauce thickens and has a nice sheen.

Serve fish corn-side up over mashed potatoes with sauce generously spooned on top.

# Pita Vera's
# Chicken Kabob

*These chicken kabobs are so sexy. This dish is full of earthy flavors, including the sweet pepper, which is imported from Lebanon. Marinate for 24 hours for the best results.*

Serves 2–4

1 pound skinless and boneless chicken breasts
1 teaspoon cinnamon
1 teaspoon sweet pepper (or allspice)
1 teaspoon minced garlic
zest of ½ orange
pinch paprika
pinch black pepper
3 tablespoons lemon juice
wooden skewers, soaked in water
vegetable or olive oil, for grilling

Wash the chicken under cold water and blot dry with a paper towel. Cut the chicken into cubes. Whisk together all remaining ingredients in a large bowl. Add the chicken and stir until seasoning is well distributed. Cover and place in refrigerator for at least 4 hours, or overnight.

Put chicken cubes on skewers and place on a clean plate. Preheat grill or grill pan on medium-high heat and brush pan with a little vegetable or olive oil. Grill chicken for about 5 minutes each side.

Pita Vera's owner, George, is a Blacksburg transplant. Having worked in the food business for years, he got a call in 2008 from his cousin (a Virginia Tech grad) encouraging him to check out the space that was once More Than Coffee. He jumped at the opportunity and created a vision of a Lebanese restaurant whose philosophy would be "order to cook," to ensure freshness. It shows.

Pita Vera's food is made using the highest quality ingredients, which are local whenever possible. The maza tray appetizer promotes a feeling of family. We passed the hummus, feta, beans, and pita back and forth while having funny and heartfelt conversation. Speaking of pita, the bread is made from a 7000-year-old recipe, so you know that it's good, and it is the lightest we've ever tried. The suguk wrap is Pita Vera's top seller, a delicious blend of ground beef and seven different Lebanese spices.

We always want to give our business to owners who care about their patrons and the quality of their food. George is a highly visible owner and puts his customers first. He says they are his bread and butter—though, we think he means his "pita and olive oil."

## Ellen Stewart's
# Farmers' Market Harvest Pork Skillet

*We love a good one-pot meal. This recipe proves that oftentimes the best dishes are the simplest. Ellen is the director of the Blacksburg Farmers' Market. All of the produce in her recipes can be found at the market on Saturday mornings all year round.*

Serves 4

2 tablespoons olive oil
4 pork chops (you may substitute 4 pork sausages)
4 cups chopped cabbage
2 cups peeled and chopped apples
1 large sweet onion, chopped
1 cup grated carrot
salt and pepper, to taste

Heat oil in a large cast-iron skillet on medium-high heat. Brown pork chops on both sides. If you are using sausages instead, brown on all sides to ensure even cooking.

Add remaining ingredients, plus ½ cup of water, and salt and pepper to taste.

Cover and simmer over medium heat, stirring occasionally and adding more water as needed. Cook until cabbage is tender, about 20 minutes.

**Cook's Note:**
We found that the addition of 1 tablespoon of red wine vinegar really enhanced the flavor of the cabbage and apples.

# Top of the Stairs'
# Ribs

*Every TOTS customer has his or her favorite TOTS moment. My first favorite has to be Valentines Day 2003 when I met my husband. But my second favorite was in April in my senior year when a few of us rolled up to the bar for an early—5 p.m.—dinner. We each ordered a grilled cheese sandwich, looked at one another and back at the bartender and said, "...and a Rail!"*

—*Krista Gallagher*

Serves 2–4

1 tablespoon garlic powder
1 tablespoon salt
1 tablespoon ground black pepper
1 tablespoon paprika
2½ pounds pork back ribs
equal parts liquid smoke and water, enough to fill a roasting pan to a depth of ¼-inch

Preheat oven to 350°F.

Mix garlic powder, salt, paprika and pepper to make a rib rub. Coat both sides of ribs with the dry seasonings. Put water and liquid smoke in bottom of a roasting pan. Place a metal rack in the bottom of a roasting pan. Place ribs on top of rack. Cover with foil and cook for 5–6 hours or until ribs are tender.

# Our Daily Bread's
# Beef Bourguignonne

*This dish truly warms the soul. We served this at a game day party in late November and it was a huge hit, especially with those meat-and-potatoes types. You may want to brown the beef in batches to ensure that it gets a nice sear, which enhances its flavor.*

Serves 6

2 tablespoons vegetable oil
½ medium yellow onion, diced
3 large carrots, sliced into 1-inch chunks
4 ounces uncooked bacon, diced
1½ pounds beef chuck, cut into 1-inch cubes
2 garlic cloves, minced
3 or 4 sprigs fresh thyme
2 bay leaves
1 bottle Burgundy wine
2 tablespoons unsalted butter
6 ounces sliced mushrooms
2 tablespoons tomato paste
2 tablespoons flour
2 tablespoons unsalted butter, softened
fresh parsley, for garnish

Pour vegetable oil into a large heavy pot or Dutch oven and cook the onions and carrots on medium heat until soft, about 8 minutes. Add the bacon and continue cooking and stirring for 8 minutes.

Sprinkle the beef with salt and pepper. Add the meat and cook, turning several times, until well-browned on all sides. Add the garlic and cook for 1 minute. Add the thyme, bay leaves, and wine. Cover, turn down the heat, and let simmer for 1½ to 2 hours.

Melt the butter in a medium skillet on medium heat and add the mushrooms. Cook until soft and add to the stew. Add tomato paste to the stew. Simmer until meat is very tender. Cook for 30 minutes more, leaving the lid off to get a more concentrated sauce. Remove and discard thyme stems and bay leaves.

To thicken the stew, mash the softened butter and flour together in a small bowl with a fork until well blended. Blend in a tablespoon of the cooking liquid, and stir this mixture back into the stew. Continue cooking for several minutes until thickened. Serve hot.

# Our Daily Bread's
# Quiche Lorraine

*As we stood in line to place our order for this quiche, we chatted it up with a woman who said she was driving through Blacksburg on her way to Florida. She simply Googled "best lunch in Blacksburg" and Our Daily Bread is what came up. We concur.*

Serves 8

1 (9-inch) pie crust
5 ounces uncooked bacon
4 ounces grated Emmentaler cheese
3 eggs
1 cup heavy cream
1 cup milk
½ teaspoon salt
¼ teaspoon pepper
dash of nutmeg

Preheat oven to 400°F.

Roll the pie dough into a large circle and place into a pie dish. Flute the edges decoratively. Place wax paper on top of the dough, lay dry beans or pie weights on it and bake for 12–15 minutes. Remove wax paper and beans, and let cool.

Decrease the oven temperature to 350°F.

Dice the bacon and cook in a small skillet until crispy. Remove bacon with a slotted spoon and place on a plate lined with a paper towel.

Whisk together eggs, cream, milk, salt, pepper, and nutmeg in a large bowl. Evenly spread out the bacon and cheese on pie crust. Pour egg mixture on top. Bake for 35 minutes or until a knife comes out clean and filling is evenly set.

# SAL's
# Seafood Pescatore

*When we walked into SAL's, we were greeted by owner Joe with a huge hug and a "you guys will make me an amazing cookbook, no?" He was very proud to give us this recipe and has every right to be. It's for one person, but we think it's a great dish for sharing. Pair with a glass of your favorite wine.*

Serves 1–2

½ pound linguine
extra-virgin olive oil
2 cloves garlic, thinly sliced
3 jumbo shrimp, shelled and deveined
8 ounces calamari, tentacles on
3 ounces white wine
3 ripe plum tomatoes, smashed (you may use canned whole tomatoes)
6 mussels, cleaned well
3 little neck clams, cleaned well
2 tablespoons chopped fresh basil
1 tablespoon chopped fresh Italian parsley
salt and pepper, to taste
red pepper flakes, to taste

Cook pasta according to package directions and keep warm until the seafood is done.

Coat a large skillet with extra-virgin olive oil and warm on medium heat. Add the garlic and cook for 1 minute. Add the shrimp and calamari to the skillet and sauté for 2 minutes.

Pour the white wine over the seafood and cook for 2 minutes. Add tomatoes, bring to a simmer, and cook for 10 minutes.

Add mussels and clams to the pan and simmer for another 8–10 minutes. Add cooked pasta, basil, parsley, salt, pepper, and red pepper flakes and toss well.

**Cook's Note:**
You can also top the pescatore with your favorite cooked filet of fish. The day we visited SAL's, he placed a delicious piece of cooked salmon right on top of the seafood pasta. He told us he uses any fish he's cooking up in the kitchen. It ... was ... divine.

# SAL's
# Chicken Bruschetta Pizza Pop

*SAL's Italian Restaurant and Pizzeria bakes these in a brick oven, though we created this using our home oven—and man, were they delicious.*

Serves 2

8 ounces pizza dough
8 ounces fresh mozzarella, shredded
2 small Roma tomatoes, diced
1 garlic clove, minced
1 tablespoon extra-virgin olive oil
1 tablespoon chopped fresh basil
salt and pepper
4 ounces cooked chicken breast

Preheat oven to 400°F.

Roll out pizza dough until it is a 10 x 10-inch square. Cut in half diagonally to form two triangles. Set aside one of them.

Spread half of the fresh mozzarella over one half of the triangle. Mix together diced tomatoes, garlic, olive oil, fresh basil, salt and pepper in a bowl. Lay half of the mixture on top of the mozzarella.

Cut the chicken into thin strips and lay half on top of the mozzarella and tomato mixture. Flip over the uncovered side of the triangle and tuck in (as you would for a popover or tart). Cut 3 slits into the top of the triangle to allow air to escape.

Repeat with second triangle, place on a greased baking sheet, and bake for about 15 minutes, or until golden brown.

# Castle's Kettle and Pub's
# Irish Coddle

*Castle's Kettle and Pub is a new Blacksburg eaterie. It's located in the same house where Kris experienced her first frat party. The house has been redone so amazingly well she can't remember what it used to look like— ahem—or, that's what she's telling her parents. This is a great Irish brunch recipe, and very traditional. Other root vegetables and various greens such as cabbage, kale, and mustard greens can be added depending on personal preference. When the coddle has 20 minutes left to cook, start to prepare the whiskey sauce.*

Serves 4

6 to 8 medium russet potatoes
2 large yellow onions
4 pork bangers (short, thick sausages)

Rinse, peel, and quarter the potatoes and onions and place them into a stew pot. Place the bangers on top of the potatoes and onions and add enough warm water to just cover the contents. Cover the pot and boil for approximately 1 hour (removing the lid after 30 minutes to reduce liquid) or until the potatoes are slightly fluffy. The salt from the bangers will flavor the potatoes. Add pepper to taste.

### For the whiskey sauce:
4 tablespoons unsalted butter
1 cup light brown sugar
3 ounces whiskey

Melt the butter in a medium saucepan over medium-low heat and whisk in the brown sugar until dissolved. Reduce heat to low, add whiskey (the whiskey may flame, so be careful) and simmer for 1 minute. The alcohol will dissolve. Remove from heat.

### To serve:
Using a slotted spoon, place the potatoes and onions into a bowl. Add approximately ⅛ cup of the cooking liquid. Slice the bangers into 1/2-inch-thick pieces, and place atop the coddle. Serve the whiskey sauce in a small individual sauce bowl on the side to dip the bangers.

# Big Al's
# Meatloaf

*Serve with potatoes and your favorite vegetable or slice thin to use on a sandwich made with toasted sourdough bread.*

Serves 4

1½ pounds ground beef
2 eggs, lightly beaten
½ cup ketchup
½ cup finely chopped onions
⅓ cup plain dry bread crumbs
1 teaspoon garlic salt
¼ teaspoon pepper

***For the topping:***
¾ cup ketchup
¼ teaspoon light brown sugar
¼ teaspoon mustard
½ teaspoon apple cider vinegar
cayenne pepper, to taste

Preheat oven to 375°F.

Mix together ground beef, eggs, ketchup, onions, bread crumbs, garlic salt, and pepper in a large bowl. Firmly pack meat mixture into a 8 x 4 x 3-inch loaf pan. Bake for 30 minutes.

Meanwhile, mix together all topping ingredients in a medium bowl. Remove the meatloaf from oven and drain excess fat. Spread topping mixture on meatloaf and bake for an additional 20 minutes.

# Side Dishes

Turner Place's Corn Pudding
Turner Place's Citrus Sweet Potatoes
Turner Place's Baked Summer Squash
Turner Place's Fried Rice
Turner Place's Maque Choux
West End Market's Grilled Asparagus with Dijon Balsamic Vinaigrette
West End Market's Broiled Tomatoes
West End Market's Roasted Garlic Whipped Potatoes
SAL's Spinach and Artichoke Sauté

*SAL's Spinach and
Artichoke Sauté
Pg. 112*

# Turner Place

T urner Place, located in Lavery Hall, will be a dining center of many firsts. It's the first dining center to be built since 1970 (Cochrane, which houses West End Market, was built in 1983). Turner Place is the first college dining center in the nation to feature a teppanyaki grill (Japanese style steakhouse). And it's the first to use solid fuel (no gas or electric) for the 5-foot char grill that is completely sourced from local hardwood, cut by Virginia Tech's own forestry club.

Turner Place is comprised of three national brands: Qdoba, Bruegger's Bagels, and Jamba Juice, as well as five unique markets. As this book went to print, the menu at Turner Place was still in development, though Assistant Director John Barrett gave us an insight into what Chef Mark Moritz had in store for the fall 2012 opening. Here's a little description of soon-to-be-popular eateries:

**Atomic Pizzeria:** The sourdough pizza crust is exclusive to Turner Place and will be made on-site. John Barrett raves about a basic pizza made with an inventive twist, the margherita, drizzled with a fig balsamic reduction.

**1872 Fire Grill:** Southern comfort foods at their best. The crunchy fried chicken is sure to be a hit, as well as the country-fried pork loin.

**Origami:** Japanese steakhouse with a teppanyaki grill and a full sushi bar. Extra wasabi, please.

**Soup Garden:** The miso dressing is to live for. Top freshly tossed salads with a protein, like marinated shrimp hot off the grill.

**Dolce e Caffè:** Made-to-order crêpes topped with fresh whipped cream, Peet's coffee, and ultracreamy gelato.

# Turner Place's
# Corn Pudding

*Butter, cheddar, and ricotta really should be their own food groups, but when married together, this corn pudding becomes an unbelievable dish. Just be prepared to feed a football team (or your hungry family) as this is a hearty side that makes a lot, and just might steal the show from your main course.*

Serves 6-8

8 tablespoons unsalted butter
1¾ pound yellow corn kernels (about 4 cups)
1 cup chopped yellow onion
4 eggs
1 cup milk
1 cup half and half
½ cup yellow cornmeal
1 cup plus 1 tablespoon ricotta cheese
2 tablespoons chopped fresh basil
1 tablespoon sugar
1 tablespoon salt
½ teaspoon pepper
¾ cup grated extra-sharp cheddar cheese, plus more for topping
large aluminum roasting pan, filled halfway with hot water

Preheat oven to 350°F.

Grease a 9 x 13-inch baking dish and set aside.

Melt butter in a very large skillet and sauté the corn and onion over medium-high heat for about 4 minutes. Cool slightly.

While the corn is cooling, whisk together the eggs, milk, and half and half in a large bowl. Slowly whisk in the cornmeal and then the ricotta. Add the basil, sugar, salt, and pepper.

Mix together the cooked corn mixture, ricotta mixture, and grated cheddar. Stir until just combined. Pour into the baking dish. Sprinkle the top with more cheddar cheese.

Place baking pan in the aluminum pan filled with hot water. Bake the pudding for 40–45 minutes until the top begins to brown, the middle is set, and a knife inserted in the center comes out clean.

Turner Place's

# Citrus Sweet Potatoes

*"When I tested this recipe, unfortunately, I had to throw what remained away or else I would have continued to eat them. They were that good—sensual, even. My husband kindly asked why I was still standing at the stove continuing to eat them, well after we had finished dinner. I was positive that with each additional bite, the decadent flavor would fade, but I was wrong. Luscious cream softens the vibrant citrus and transforms ordinary potatoes into something that will not allow you to put your fork down."*

—*Krista Gallagher*

Serves 6–8

pan spray
zest of 2 oranges
zest of 2 lemons
¼ cup orange juice concentrate, thawed
1 tablespoon salt
3 pounds sweet potatoes, thinly sliced
3 pounds russet potatoes, thinly sliced
2 cups heavy cream

Preheat oven to 350°F.

Spray a baking sheet with pan spray.

Spread the zests evenly over the prepared pan. Evenly add the orange juice concentrate and the salt. Alternate layers of sweet and russet potatoes. Pour the heavy cream over the potatoes. Cover the pan and bake for 30 minutes. Remove the cover and bake an additional 15 minutes, or until potatoes are fork tender.

*Turner Place's*

# Baked Summer Squash

*We made this with vegetables we purchased at the Blacksburg Farmers' Market—fresh, simple, and the perfect accompaniment to grilled chicken or fish.*

Serves 6–8

4 tablespoons olive oil
2 pounds yellow onions, thinly sliced
5 pounds yellow squash, sliced ¼-inch-thick
1 pound red pepper, sliced ½-inch-thick
1 tablespoon salt
½ teaspoon pepper
1 cup shredded Parmesan cheese

Preheat oven to 350°F.

Heat the oil in a large skillet. Add the onions and sauté until slightly caramelized. Add the squash and peppers, and cook for 5 minutes. Season with the salt and pepper.

Transfer vegetables to a baking sheet and top with the cheese. Bake for 20 minutes.

# Turner Place's
# Fried Rice

*Ginger. Ginger is exactly the ingredient fried rice has been missing all these years. Chef Mark Moritz also uses safflower oil for its high smoke point, which allows it to get perfectly hot without compromising the nutritional integrity or flavor of the dish.*

Serves 4

4¾ ounces white rice (about ¾ cup)
2 tablespoons safflower oil
2 tablespoons brunoised carrots (small cubed)
3 tablespoons scallions, white and green parts, separated
¾ teaspoon fresh ginger, minced
1½ teaspoons garlic, minced
1 large egg
2 teaspoons safflower oil
¼ teaspoon salt
3 tablespoons soy sauce

Cook the rice in 1½ cups water according to package directions. Once done, break rice apart into small pieces.

Heat a wok or a large skillet on medium-high heat until very hot. Add 2 tablespoons safflower oil and swirl it. Add the carrot, white part of the scallion, ginger, and garlic, and sauté quickly for about 2 minutes.

Whisk together the egg, 2 teaspoons safflower oil, and salt in a small bowl. Add the egg mixture to the wok and let cook for about 1 minute, then scramble.

Add the cooked rice to the wok and stir fry until the rice reaches 165°F for 15 seconds. Add the soy sauce and toss together. Garnish with the green portion of the scallion and serve.

# Turner Place's
# Maque Choux

*This Cajun side dish is a staple in New Orleans and fits perfectly into Turner Place's 1872 Fire Grill, a high-end grill station with Southern flare. Maque choux pairs well with the newest dining hall's country fried pork loin.*

Serves 4–6

6 ounces uncooked bacon, cut into strips
4 tablespoons unsalted butter
1 small yellow onion, small diced
1 medium green bell pepper, small diced
2 tablespoons small diced jalapeño peppers
1½ teaspoons minced garlic
1 pound corn kernels
¾ cup tomato concasse (peeled, seeded, and diced tomatoes)*
⅛ teaspoon cayenne pepper
½ tablespoon chicken base
2 cups heavy cream
1 pound collard greens, cleaned and chopped
2 russet potatoes, diced
¼ teaspoon salt
dash of pepper

Cook bacon in a heavy stockpot or Dutch oven until crisp, drain on paper towels, crumble, and set aside. Discard all but 2 tablespoons of bacon fat. Melt butter in the same pan over medium heat.

Add onion, green pepper, jalapeño peppers, and garlic, and sauté for 5 minutes until onion has softened. Stir in corn, tomatoes, and cayenne pepper, and cook for 5 more minutes, stirring occasionally.

Add chicken base and cream. Reduce heat to medium-low. Add the collard greens and potatoes. Cover the pan partially and cook until the liquid is reduced by two-thirds, about 45 minutes, stirring occasionally. Remove from heat, stir in crumbled bacon, and serve.

*We used canned diced tomatoes for the tomato concasse.

# Grilled Asparagus with Dijon Balsamic Vinaigrette

*Any ordinary dining hall can steam a floret of broccoli. Once again, West End Market exceeds its students' expectations with this flavorful and healthy vegetable side dish. This recipe goes to show that you don't need to drench vegetables with butter or cheese to make them taste good.*

Serves 4

14 ounces asparagus
1 tablespoon olive oil
pinch each of salt and black pepper
balsamic vinaigrette, recipe follows

Preheat grill or grill pan to medium-high heat.

Wash asparagus and trim approximately 2 inches from the woody ends of each. Transfer to a clean plate and coat with olive oil. Season with salt and pepper. Carefully lay the asparagus on the grill or grill pan and cook for approximately 5 minutes, turning frequently to ensure they do not burn.

**For the balsamic vinaigrette:**
½ cup balsamic vinegar
1 tablespoon Dijon mustard
1 tablespoon minced garlic
1 tablespoon minced shallot
1 tablespoon lemon juice
1 teaspoon salt
½ teaspoon ground black pepper
1 teaspoon sugar
¼ cup olive oil

Combine first eight ingredients in a blender or food processor and pulse several times until all ingredients are combined. Slowly drizzle in olive oil and lightly stir.

Pour enough on a platter to lightly cover the bottom and top with asparagus. Serve the extra vinaigrette on the side.

**To serve:**
Coat bottom of a platter with balsamic vinaigrette and place grilled asparagus on top.

# West End Market's
# Broiled Tomatoes

*This is a quick and easy side dish that is as beautiful as it is wholesome. The best time to make this is during the summer months when tomatoes are bright red and juicy.*

Serves 4–6

3 large tomatoes
1 teaspoon salt
pinch ground black pepper
1¼ teaspoon Italian seasoning
1 tablespoon olive oil
½ cup shredded mozzarella cheese
½ cup shredded provolone cheese

Preheat oven to 350°F.

Wash the tomatoes. Cut tomatoes in half. Remove and discard the core and pulp of each half using a melon baller or a metal spoon. Place tomato halves in a large baking dish.

Combine both of the cheeses in a small bowl. Season each tomato half with the salt, pepper, and Italian seasoning. Drizzle with olive oil and bake for 10–15 minutes until the tomatoes are cooked and slightly soft to touch. Remove briefly from the oven and increase the oven temperature to broil.

Top each half with a tablespoon of the cheese. Place pan in the upper half of the oven and broil until the cheese is golden brown.

# West End Market's
# Roasted Garlic Whipped Potatoes

*We were straight-up dumbfounded to learn that this recipe called for a paltry amount of milk, not a gallon of heavy cream that we could only assume was essential for potatoes as creamy as these. Serve hot alongside West End's London broil and top both with the mushroom gravy.*

Serves 8

**For the roasted garlic:**
1 ounce peeled fresh garlic (about 6 cloves)
2 tablespoons unsalted butter, melted

Preheat oven to 275°F.

Toss the garlic with the melted butter in a small bowl. Transfer garlic to a baking sheet lined with aluminum foil and bake uncovered for 15–20 minutes, or until golden. Remove from oven and while still warm, mash the garlic with a fork or a food processor. Chill until ready to use.

**For the potatoes:**
2 pounds, 10 ounces russet potatoes
4 tablespoons unsalted butter, melted
¾ cup plus 3 tablespoons 2% milk
1½ teaspoons Kosher salt
¼ teaspoon ground black pepper

Place potatoes in a large stockpot and cover with water. Bring to a boil and cook for approximately 30 minutes, or until very tender. Drain the potatoes in a colander. Place them in the bowl of a standing mixer fitted with a wire whip. Add melted butter, milk, salt, pepper, and roasted garlic. Mix on medium-high speed until thoroughly whipped. Serve hot.

**Cook's Note:**
Cook peeled potatoes whole in order to retain both the starch and integrity of the potato.

# SAL's
# Spinach and Artichoke Sauté

*This flavorful side dish proves that you don't need crazy ingredients or a complicated recipe to make something delicious. Pair this with any meal or eat it by itself straight from the skillet.*

Serves 4-6

extra-virgin olive oil
3 cloves garlic, sliced
1 pound fresh spinach
12 artichoke hearts, quartered (frozen or canned)
salt and pepper, to taste

Coat a large skillet with olive oil and place on medium-low heat. Once hot, sauté sliced garlic until soft, about 1–2 minutes.

Add the spinach and artichoke hearts and cook for about 2 minutes, until spinach is completely wilted. Remove from heat. Season with salt and pepper.

# Tailgating

The Clubhouse Tailgate's Drunken Pork with Sour Cream Bourbon Sauce

Rob's Armadillo Tails

Luther Burgers

The Pilson's Chicken Wing Dip

Kris' Cheesy Hot Pigs in a Blanket with Mustard Dipping Sauce

Bonnie's Hot Crab Dip

Krista's Stromboli with Crunchy Topping

The Lawler's Cowboy Beans

The Hoyt's Asparagus Bundles

Susan Pilson's Chocolate Chip Rum Cake

The Clubhouse Tailgate's Wild Turkey® Fudge

The Poole's Caramel Apple Dip

Game Day Turkey Legs

Katie's Garlic Chicken Bites

Harrison's Maroon Martini

Tom's Tailgate Beer

The Red Eye

Karen's Hot Gobbler

Maroon and Orange Jello Shots

*Tailgating*

T ailgating before any home football game is quite possibly one of Virginia Tech's greatest traditions. It's hard to describe the feeling of pulling into the Virginia Tech campus on a game weekend. You can feel the rumble of excitement in your bones, even the day before the game. "I'll be busy tomorrow—game day," is a phrase that you hear from every local restaurateur. Students are decked out in maroon and orange long before the tailgating begins. RVs pull in on Friday, getting prepared for Saturday's game, and the die-hards begin cooking up their dishes before the opposing team has even woken up. You see, tailgating at Virginia Tech is an art form; one that not many understand... unless they're Hokies.

The scene in every parking lot on campus is vibrant. Maroon and orange are everywhere; the sound of the chant "Let's go!" followed by "Hokies!" is heard from a mile away, and the smell of just-ignited charcoal grills all remind us, it's our favorite time of year again: football season.

Everyone has a favorite spot (far right side of the commuter lot), a favorite beverage (Wild Turkey®), favorite snack foods (burgers with bacon and cheddar), favorite games (corn hole), and a favorite chair (a VT one, of course).

The parking lot at the back end of campus is jammed packed with RVs and SUVs. The lot across from Cassell Coliseum and Lane Stadium is even worse, and by "worse," we mean, even better. These folks have a VIP spot, thanks to being or knowing a Hokie Club member. They could spit on Lane Stadium from their tailgating locale. Not that they would want to. This highly coveted area makes for a timely entry into the stadium to jump up and down to the tune of Metallica's "Enter Sandman."

Who better to tell stories of tailgates past than the all-star tailgaters themselves? On the following pages, you'll find a variety of traditions from several serious Virginia Tech alums.

"Football games are the best occasions for tailgates. Unfortunately, football season does not last very long. Other acceptable occasions for tailgating are basketball tournaments, automobile races, baseball games, hockey matches, golf tournaments, tennis matches, soccer matches, horse races, rodeos, wrestling exhibitions, badminton matches, croquet tournaments, triathlons, swimming meets, poker games, squash matches, dog shows, demolition derbies, hunting season, cricket matches, bicycle tours, Olympiads, women's mud and oil wrestling, theatric premieres, building demolitions, concerts, sunrises and sunsets, Virginia Tech joining the ACC, anniversaries of Virginia Tech joining the ACC, and any other reason anybody can come up with."

—The Clubhouse Tailgate

# The Clubhouse Tailgate's
# Drunken Pork with Sour Cream Bourbon Sauce

*The Clubhouse Tailgate was established in 1998 and has grown steadily since then, practicing a pregame "communion" toast that now involves about 40–50 people. Today, a typical tailgate will feature five decades of Virginia Tech graduates gathering together to enjoy the fellowship and Hokie hospitality that the Clubhouse is known for.*

Serves 4–6

⅓ cup Wild Turkey 101®
¼ cup firmly packed light brown sugar
½ cup low-sodium soy sauce
2½ pounds pork tenderloin
large sealable plastic bag

Whisk together Wild Turkey®, brown sugar, and soy sauce in a small bowl to form marinade. Place pork tenderloin and marinade in plastic storage bag and refrigerate for 30–60 minutes. Meanwhile, preheat smoker. Remove tenderloin from bag and discard marinade. Place in smoker and smoke until internal temperature reaches 145°F. Alternatively, preheat oven to 400°F, drain the marinade and place the tenderloin in an aluminum foil lined roasting pan. Roast for around 50 minutes, or until done. Let pork rest for 10 minutes so the juices redistribute inside the meat. Slice pork and serve with sour cream bourbon sauce.

**For the sour cream bourbon sauce:**
1 tablespoon extra-virgin olive oil
3 scallions, chopped (white and light green parts)
¼ cup Wild Turkey 101®
¾ cup sour cream
2 teaspoons honey
2 teaspoons Dijon mustard
¼ teaspoon salt
freshly ground black pepper, to taste

Heat olive oil in small sauté pan on medium-low heat. Add scallions and cook for 30 seconds. Carefully add Wild Turkey 101® (use caution as it can flame up; allow flames to dwindle). Cook until scallions are translucent, about 3–5 minutes. Remove from heat and let cool slightly. Combine cooled scallions with remaining ingredients in a small bowl. Season to taste with additional salt and pepper.

# Rob's
# Armadillo Tails

*The Quillen tailgate, complete with a tricked-out trailer that includes beer taps coming out of the sides, is definitely one to visit on game day. With the pregame show on TV and, not one, but two gigantic grills, what more could you want?*

Serves 4–6

12 jalapeño peppers
8 ounces cream cheese, softened
8 slices cooked bacon, chopped
4 pounds raw pork sausage

Slice each jalapeño in half, lengthwise, keeping stems intact.

Remove and discard the seeds and fill one side of each pepper half with 1 tablespoon cream cheese placing a piece of cooked bacon on top of the cream cheese.

Ball sausage around the whole stuffed pepper, leaving the stem out on one end. Grill or fry in a hot skillet with oil until the outer layer of sausage is browned and cooked through.

## Cook's Note:
This recipe makes 24 very large tails. If that seems like too much for your crowd, the recipe can easily be cut in half—but when is too much tail ever a bad thing?

Tailgating 122

# Luther Burgers

*Courtesy of the Quillen tailgate, this burger is bold. We're not sure anyone can finish a whole Luther burger, but with its salty/sweet combo, it's definitely worth a shot.*

Serves 4

1 pound ground beef, formed into ¼ pound patties
4 slices American cheese
4 slices cheddar cheese
4 slices cooked bacon
8 glazed donuts

Preheat grill.

Cook hamburger patties to desired doneness. While still on the grill, top with cheeses and let melt. Remove from grill and place on clean plate. Place one slice of bacon on each pattie.

Place donuts on grill and cook for 1 minute, until warm. Remove from grill and place on a clean plate. Place hamburger pattie on a donut and top each with remaining donut to form a sandwich. Flatten lightly with a spatula.

# The Pilson's
## Chicken Wing Dip

*The Pilsons (Susan Pilson is the Martha Stewart of tailgating) know how to do a tailgate, that's for sure. With a spread that should be in* Southern Living *magazine, this is no typical parking-lot fare. The table is heaving with food such as chicken wing dip (served in a heated football dish, of course), chocolate chip rum cake, Brunswick stew, barbeque chicken, Mediterranean pasta salad, and ham biscuits to name a few—just a very few.*

Serves 4–6

2 (12.5-ounce) cans chunk chicken, drained
¾ cup wing sauce
1 (8-ounce) package cream cheese, softened
1 (8-ounce) bottle bleu cheese dressing
1 (8-ounce) bottle ranch dressing
1 pound grated cheddar cheese

Heat chicken and wing sauce together in a large saucepan on medium heat until warmed through. Add remaining ingredients and stir until the cheese is melted. Serve hot with crackers or crusty bread.

# Kris'
# Cheesy Hot Pigs in a Blanket
## with Mustard Dipping Sauce

*What is game day without pigs in a blanket? Opt out of the traditional and serve these spicy little guys while you watch Beamer do his thing.*

Makes 32

2 packages crescent roll dough
32 cocktail franks
1 cup shredded cheddar cheese
1 (11-ounce) can sliced jalapeños

Preheat oven to 375°F.

Spray baking sheet with nonstick cooking spray.

Separate dough from both packages of crescent rolls and into 16 triangles. Cut each triangle in half. Place cocktail frank on widest end of each triangle. Sprinkle cheese and jalapeños over the frank. Roll each piece up tightly.

Place on cookie sheet and bake 12–15 minutes, or until golden brown.

**For the dipping sauce:**
½ cup Dijon mustard
2 tablespoons sour cream

Whisk together and chill until ready to serve.

GO HOKIES!

FREIGHTLINER

# Bonnie's
# Hot Crab Dip

*The combo of flavors in this dip makes it a fan favorite, courtesy of the Martin/Osborne Tailgate.*

Serves 8

2 (8-ounce) packages cream cheese, softened
1 cup sour cream
4 tablespoons mayonnaise
3 teaspoons Worcestershire sauce
1 teaspoon dry mustard
¼ teaspoon garlic powder
½ teaspoon lemon juice
1 cup grated sharp cheddar cheese
1 pound lump crabmeat, picked over for shells

Preheat oven to 325°F.

Grease an 8 x 8-inch baking dish.

Beat cream cheese in the bowl of an electric mixer on medium speed for about 2 minutes. Add sour cream, mayonnaise, Worcestershire sauce, mustard, garlic powder, lemon juice, and cheddar cheese, and mix until well blended, about 2 more minutes. Fold crab meat into mixture with a rubber spatula.

Spoon into greased dish and bake for 30–45 minutes until bubbly. Serve hot with crackers or tortilla chips.

# Stromboli with Crunchy Topping

*Why is it always the simplest recipe that is the biggest hit? This stromboli is a staple at every game party the Gallagher's host. We insist you use fresh Parmigiano-Reggiano. Don't even think about using Parmesan out of the can.*

Serves 6–8

1 pizza dough (alternatively, 1 package store-bought pizza dough)
1 (8-ounce) package pepperoni
2 packages sliced provolone cheese
extra-virgin olive oil
marinara sauce, for dipping (optional)

**For the crunchy topping:**
½ cup grated Parmigiano-Reggiano
1 teaspoon Italian seasoning
1 teaspoon sesame seeds
½ teaspoon garlic powder
pinch of red pepper flakes

Preheat oven to 350°F.

Line a baking sheet with parchment paper. On a lightly floured board, roll out pizza dough to a 10 x 12-inch rectangle. Cut into quarters. On each quarter, layer 2 slices of provolone and enough pepperoni to cover the dough. Roll dough diagonally to form a log. Repeat with remaining pieces of dough. Brush each with olive oil.

Combine all topping ingredients in a small bowl and sprinkle over each stromboli roll. Bake for 20–25 minutes, or until golden brown. Let cool 5 minutes. Transfer to a cutting board and slice diagonally. Serve hot.

"Early on the day of my first tailgating experience, ESPN Game Day's Lee Corso picked Virginia Tech to lose, a prediction that created furor among us Hokies. At each of the tailgates I went to, it was all anyone wanted to talk about—that and the impending thunderstorm that could prevent us from proving Lee Corso wrong. 20 minutes before the game, the wind picked up and the sky darkened. Even so, thousands of deeply devoted fans quickly packed up their parties and hoofed it into the stadium as if ignoring the signs would send the storm someplace else (like Charlottesville). At just about kickoff time lightning struck. The game was cancelled. Word spread that there was a car on fire. Turns out, that car was Lee Corso's. Corso later joked by asking, 'Was God a Hokie?' Although the weather did not permit a return to the tailgate, I ended up with a great memory of my first tailgate."

# The Lawler's
# Cowboy Beans

*"There is a really cool tradition called Communion. At 10 a.m. in the RV lot by the airport, everybody is out there. Shots of liquor (Wild Turkey®) are lined up in a "VT" shape on the table and each person goes out to find a fan from the opposing team and gets them to take a shot—it's a great way to promote good sportsmanship. My mom makes cowboy beans, which is sort of like chili and is always good for those cold game days. Tailgating is a full weekend event for our family and friends. Arriving Friday morning in our motor home, the first order of events is decorating the interior and exterior of the RV with flags, helmets, footballs, and a canopy. Food preparation began at home and continues on through Saturday morning by cooking a casserole, chili, and Swedish meatballs. The menu also includes deviled eggs, ham biscuits, and veggie or fruit trays. Entertainment includes games, throwing footballs, and watching game day via satellite. Some tailgaters stay overnight, but all depart by Sunday morning. A good time is had by all as long as we have won the game!"*

—Mike Lawler

1 (19-ounce) can pinto beans, undrained
1 (15.75-ounce) can pork and beans, undrained
1 (15.5-ounce) can red kidney beans, undrained
1 (15.5-ounce) can white beans beans, undrained
olive oil
1 pound ground beef
1 cup chopped yellow onion
1 cup chopped green pepper
1 cup barbeque sauce

Place all undrained beans in a crockpot, turn on heat, and do not stir.

Pour 2–3 tablespoons of olive oil in a large skillet on medium heat and add ground beef, onion, and pepper. Cook until meat is browned and vegetables are tender. Add to the crockpot on top of the beans. Do not stir.

Pour barbecue sauce evenly on top of ground beef mixture. Don't you dare stir.

Cook on high heat until bubbly, about 1½ hours. Lower heat to low and cook for another 3 hours.

Stir well (finally!) and serve hot.

# The Hoyt's
## Asparagus Bundles

*These asparagus bundles definitely add elegance to an unsuspecting tailgating party. Who would've thought a vegetable dish would be the first to disappear at the Hoyt tailgate?*

1 bundle thick asparagus, ends trimmed, blanched until tender but firm
juice of 1 lemon
slices of serrano ham or prosciutto
freshly grated Parmigiano-Reggiano

Squeeze lemon juice on cooked asparagus. Wrap each piece with ham. Place on a clean plate and sprinkle with cheese. Refrigerate until ready to eat.

**Cook's Note:**
This dish can be made a day in advance.

## Susan Pilson's
# Chocolate Chip Rum Cake

*This cake has won local awards, and we can definitely see why. It is truly decadent. This dessert is moist (contains rum), full of flavor (rum), and takes little time to prepare (rum). Touchdown!*

1 box yellow cake mix
1 (5.1-ounce) box instant chocolate pudding mix
4 eggs
1 (8-ounce) container sour cream
½ cup vegetable oil
¼ cup rum
6 ounces semisweet chocolate chips
6 ounces chopped walnuts or pecans
1 teaspoon vanilla extract

Preheat oven to 350°F.

Grease a bundt pan.

Mix all ingredients together in a large bowl and pour into prepared pan. Bake for 1 hour, or until a cake tester comes out clean. Remove from oven and let cool in the pan for 15 minutes. Invert onto a clean cake plate. Spoon on glaze.

### For the glaze:
1 cup sugar
¼ cup hot water
8 tablespoons unsalted butter
¼ cup rum

Mix ingredients together in a saucepan. Cook on high heat until sugar is melted, about 2–3 minutes, stirring constantly. Pour over the cake as soon as it is removed from the pan, still hot.

# The Clubhouse Tailgate's
# Wild Turkey® Fudge

*Wild Turkey® bourbon casually makes its way into this insane dessert. Take the Clubhouse Tailgate's advice and double this recipe. Feel free to substitute your favorite nut for the almonds.*

> "Post-game tailgates are much better following Tech wins, but what the hell, there is still food and drink to be consumed."
> —The Clubhouse Tailgate

Serves 8-10

2 cups semisweet chocolate chips
1 (14-ounce) can sweetened condensed milk
¼ cup bourbon, or more to taste
½ teaspoon orange extract
3 ounces slivered almonds

Combine chocolate chips and condensed milk in large saucepan on medium-low heat and cook until chocolate melts. Stir until smooth. Alternatively, place chocolate and milk in a large bowl and cook in microwave in 30-second intervals until chocolate is melted.

Add bourbon and orange extract to mixture, and mix until well combined. Add additional bourbon to taste.

Grease 8-inch square pan and sprinkle bottom of pan with nuts. Pour mixture into pan and let stand until firm or chill in refrigerator.

**Cook's Note:**
It is best to make a second pan as one will not suffice.

# The Poole's
# Caramel Apple Dip

*"Game day Saturday usually starts around 7:00 a.m. if it's a noon game, or 8:00 a.m. if it's a later game. I usually wake everyone up by shouting 'It's game day, bitches!' After running to the grocery store for some last-minute beers and ice, we like to get to the parking lot and scope out the perfect corner spot with lots of grass so that we can set up games like cornhole and beer pong.*

*"Breakfast usually consists of ham biscuits, mimosas, and screwdrivers, or Gatorade (for those who have had a rough night). Later, we pull out the grill for hot dogs, chicken on a stick, bratwurst, and sausages. For the last home game of each year, we usually go big and bring out the deep fryer to fry a turkey. It is gobbled up right away.*

*Drinks at the tailgate include bourbon, champagne (for the ladies), and of course lots of beer. My mom usually drinks Virginia Tech wine out of a Virginia Tech glass to keep in the spirit of things. After each game, whether it's at noon or at night, we head to TOTS TOTS TOTS for victory Rails on the deck. Tailgating helps us relive our four years at Tech in two short days!"*

—Harrison Poole

Serves 10-12

1 (8-ounce) container whipped cream cheese
1 jar caramel sauce
1 toffee chocolate candy bar, crushed
sliced apples and ginger snaps, for dipping

Spread cream cheese in a shallow dish and top with caramel sauce. Sprinkle with crushed candy bar.

# Game Day Turkey Legs

*Courtesy of, um ... the Hokiebird? A Virginia Tech tradition at its finest. Don't worry about looking elegant while eating these, just go for it.*

Serves 6

6 turkey legs
½ cup packed brown sugar
½ cup Kosher salt
6 teaspoons liquid smoke
water, as needed to cover

Rinse turkey legs, blot dry with a paper towel, and place in a large bowl, set aside.

Dissolve brown sugar in about 3 cups of water in a medium bowl. Pour over drumsticks. Dissolve salt in another 3 cups of water in the bowl that you used to dissolve the sugar. Pour over drumsticks. Add liquid smoke. Add more water, if needed, to cover the drumsticks. Toss gently to combine. Cover bowl with plastic wrap and refrigerate overnight.

To grill, spray cold rack with vegetable oil spray (make sure rack is not over flame). Place used brine in grill-safe pan, and place pan between charcoal and legs of grill. This will help to keep the turkey moist while grilling.

Grill drumsticks about 7 minutes per side until lightly browned, turning often. Grill about 1 hour more, until tender. Add more water to brine pan as needed.

# Katie's
# Garlic Chicken Bites

*This recipe comes from one of our student interns. She got the recipe from her aunt and makes them for almost every game—always a hit.*

Serves 4–6

1 pound boneless, skinless chicken breasts cut into bite-sized pieces
¼ cup olive oil
4 cloves garlic, minced
¼ teaspoon black pepper
½ cup breadcrumbs
¼ teaspoon cayenne pepper

Place chicken, olive oil, garlic, and pepper in a large bowl or ziplock bag, and refrigerate for 30 minutes.

Preheat oven to 475°F.

Mix breadcrumbs with cayenne pepper in a medium bowl. Remove chicken from the container and discard the marinade. Dredge chicken in breadcrumb mixture and arrange on a baking sheet in one layer.

Bake for 15 minutes and then turn chicken with a spatula and bake for 5 more minutes until they are a golden brown. Serve with dipping sauce.

### For the dipping sauce:
8 tablespoons spicy barbeque sauce
2 tablespoons regular barbeque sauce
hot sauce, to taste

Whisk all ingredients together in a small bowl.

# Harrison's
## *Maroon Martini*

Makes 1

1 part vodka
1 part pomegranate juice
orange slices

Combine vodka and pomegranate juice. Pour over ice or shake with a cocktail shaker to chill. Garnish with orange slice.

Tom's
# Tailgate Beer

*Courtesy of the Clubhouse tailgate, this is, hands-down, the most fool proof (recipe?) in this book. Take care to chill for the directed amount of time. You'll thank us.*

1 case of your favorite beer
3 bags of ice (cubes)
1 cooler

Remove beer from cardboard holder. Place beer in cooler and intermingle with ice cubes.

Chill for 45 minutes and consume.

# The Red Eye

*"You can feel good about the morning nutrition of this drink—vitamins, minerals ... beer."*

—*Karen Torgersen*

Makes 1

1 shot spicy tomato juice
1 beer

Mix beer and tomato juice together in a large glass.

Pat yourself on the back and think of all of the great vitamins and minerals you are consuming so early in the day.

# Karen's
# Hot Gobbler

*Karen Torgersen is a tailgating pro, so when she told us that this is her favorite way to kickstart a game day morning, well, who were we to argue?*

Makes 1

1 shot Wild Turkey®
1 cup freshly brewed coffee

Pour hot coffee into a mug. Mix in Wild Turkey® while chanting "Hokie, Hokie, Hokie hi!"

# Maroon and Orange Jello Shots

*This recipe proves that you don't have to be an official alumni to love all things Virginia Tech. Jordan Rae Smith is the fiancé of Matt Kelly ('05) who has converted her into a die-hard Hokie fan except on the days when they take on her own alma mater, Wake Forest. We found her blog, "Alice In the Kitchen," and pictures of these jello shots while browsing on Pinterest. If someone had told us we would be testing out jello shots for a cookbook, we probably would have written one much sooner.*

Makes 50

50 disposable 2-ounce shot cups with lids, available at most party supply stores

**Maroon Layer:**
2 (3-ounce) boxes black cherry gelatin
2 cups boiling water
2 cups vodka

**Note:** Although gelatin is available in a 6-ounce box, because you are making five-layer shots with a maroon layer on top and bottom, it works better to make separate batches of maroon gelatin at the beginning and end of the process.

Empty black cherry gelatin into a medium bowl and pour 1 cup boiling water over and stir until thoroughly dissolved. Cool to room temperature and then stir in 1 cup of vodka. Using a tablespoon to ensure uniform layers, pour the mixture into shot glasses or disposable shot cups (obligatory for a tailgate). Refrigerate for at least 30 minutes, or until slightly set. This is very important as the maroon and orange layers will bleed into the white layers if they are not adequately set.

**White Layer:**
½ cup cold water
2 envelopes unflavored gelatin
1½ cups boiling water
1 (14-ounce) can condensed milk

For the first white layer, pour ½ cup cold water into a bowl. Sprinkle 2 envelopes of unflavored gelatin into the water. After the gelatin blooms, add 1½ cups boiling water and stir to dissolve. Add the can condensed milk. Stir and cool to room temperature. Spoon over the chilled maroon layer using a tablespoon. You will only need half of this mixture to make the first white layer. The white mixture will not set as long as it is kept at room temperature while you are preparing the orange layer.

### Orange Layer:
1 (3-ounce) box orange gelatin
1 cup boiling water
1 cup vodka (you may use orange or vanilla flavored vodka)

Empty orange gelatin into a medium bowl and pour 1 cup of boiling water over and stir until thoroughly dissolved. Cool to room temperature, then stir in the vodka. Spoon mixture over the white layer.

### Final two layers:
Spoon a tablespoon of the remaining white mixture into each cup. Mix remaining ingredients for the final maroon layer, allowing adequate time to cool before spooning on top. Refrigerate until ready to serve. Shots will keep in the refrigerator for up to five days.

# Sweets, Treats, Hokie-Inspired Eats

West End Market's Créme Brulée

West End Market's Strawberry Banana Smoothie

West End Market's Sugar Cookies

Lefty's Bourbon Pecan Pie

Bollo's Scones

Gillie's Banana Walnut French Toast

622 North's Cucumber Cooler Martini

Our Daily Bread's Almond Macarons

The Farmhouse's Chocolate Chess Sundae Pie

Peg Morse's Holiday Peppermint Ice Cream Sandwiches

Next Door Bake Shop's Coconut Cupcakes with Coconut Frosting

The Beamer's Cola Cake

Dr. Frank Conforti's Chocolate Chip Angel Food Cake

Maroon and Orange Cookies

Cramming for Finals Cookie Dough Cupcakes

Rail Brownies

Hokie Pokie Bars

Hokie Tartlets

Hokie Cupcakes

*Hokie Cupcakes*
*Pg. 178*

# West End Market's
## Crème Brulée

*It may be safe to say that West End Market was the first and perhaps only dining hall to serve college students this decadent dessert. Make sure you strain the custard through a fine-mesh sieve before chilling, or you may end up with sweet scrambled eggs—not awesome.*

Serves 4

2 cups heavy cream, divided
⅓ cup sugar
pinch of salt
1 vanilla bean, split in half lengthwise
6 egg yolks
4 tablespoons sugar

Combine 1 cup cream with the sugar and salt in a large saucepan over medium-low heat. Run a small knife down the vanilla bean to scrape the seeds into the cream. Add the vanilla bean pod to the cream. Bring to a simmer. When small bubbles begin to form around the edge of the pan, remove from heat. Let steep for 15–20 minutes to infuse flavors. Discard the vanilla bean pod.

Whisk together the remaining 1 cup cream and egg yolks in a medium bowl. Slowly whisk egg mixture into the vanilla-infused cream. Strain through a fine mesh sieve into a large bowl. Cover with plastic wrap and chill in the refrigerator for 6 hours.

Preheat oven to 300°F.

Divide the cream mixture evenly into 4 ramekins. Transfer ramekins to a 2-inch deep casserole dish. Add hot water to the casserole dish, up to the top edge of the ramekins, taking care not to spill water over cream.

Bake for approximately 40 minutes, or until the custard is evenly set. Remove from oven and chill in refrigerator for 2 hours.

### To serve:
Top each crème brulée with 1 tablespoon sugar and carefully caramelize using a kitchen torch. Alternatively, place tray of crème brulées under the broiler until sugar is caramelized.

# West End Market's
# Strawberry Banana Smoothie

*This smoothie was always a post-gym workout staple, and by "workout" we mean walking the indoor track while looking at boys and catching up on gossip.*

Serves 1 (20-ounce) smoothie

12 ounces frozen strawberries
4 ounces sliced frozen bananas
6 ounces crushed ice

Place strawberries along with juice and bananas in a blender. Top with the ice and puree on high speed until creamy, about 60–90 seconds.

# West End Market's
# Sugar Cookies

*You can find these cookies at West End Market's Wired. They are so popular that West End sells them by the pack several times a year. Christmas presents? Yes, please.*

Makes 25

3 cups flour
1½ teaspoon baking powder
½ teaspoon baking soda
¾ teaspoon salt
1 cup unsalted butter, room temperature
2 tablespoons light corn syrup
1¼ cups sugar
¼ cup cream cheese
1 teaspoon vanilla extract
¼ teaspoon almond extract
1 large egg
¾ cup raw sugar

Preheat oven to 350°F.

Line a baking sheet with parchment paper.

Combine the flour, baking powder, baking soda, and salt in a medium bowl. Set aside.

Cream the butter, corn syrup, sugar, and cream cheese until light and fluffy in a mixer fitted with the paddle attachment, about 3 minutes. Beat in vanilla and almond extracts. Add the egg. Scrape down the sides of the bowl and beat again until well incorporated. Reduce the speed to low and add the flour mixture until just combined. Don't overmix.

Place the raw sugar into a bowl. Scoop the dough out into 1½ ounce balls. Roll each ball in the raw sugar and place them 1½ inches apart on baking sheet. Flatten each ball lightly with your fingers.

Bake for 10–12 minutes, or until lightly browned. Remove from the oven and let cool in the pan for 5 minutes. Transfer cookies to a wire rack and let cool completely.

**Cook's Note:**
Maroon and orange sprinkles can (and should) be used in place of the raw sugar.

Lefty's

# Bourbon Pecan Pie

The dessert selection at Lefty's is always enticing. We adore the bourbon cream atop a warm piece of this pie.

### For the pie crust:
1¼ cups all-purpose flour
½ tablespoon sugar
½ teaspoon salt
½ cup chilled unsalted butter, cut into ½-inch cubes
3 tablespoons (or more) ice water

Mix flour, sugar, and salt in a food processor by pulsing several times. Add butter and pulse several times until butter is the size of peas. Add 3 tablespoons water and pulse a few times until moist clumps form, adding ½ tablespoon at a time if dough is dry. Carefully remove the blade and dump dough onto a lightly floured surface. Gather dough into ball and flatten into disk. Wrap in plastic and refrigerate at least 1 hour. Soften slightly at room temperature before rolling.

Roll out dough on lightly floured surface to a diameter of 13 inches. Transfer to 9-inch glass pie dish. Trim overhang to ½-inch. Fold overhang under and crimp edges decoratively. Refrigerate 1 hour.

Preheat oven to 375°F. Line pie crust with foil. Fill with dried beans or pie weights. Bake until crust edges begin to brown and crust is set, about 15 minutes. Remove foil and beans. Poke dough with fork in several areas and continue to bake until golden brown, about 5 more minutes. Remove from oven and let cool on a rack. Maintain oven temperature.

### For the filling:
1 cup firmly packed light brown sugar
1 cup light corn syrup
¼ cup unsalted butter, melted
3 large eggs
3 tablespoons bourbon
1 tablespoon orange zest
1 teaspoon vanilla extract
¼ teaspoon salt
2 cups pecan halves, toasted

Whisk together brown sugar, corn syrup, and melted butter in a large bowl. Whisk in eggs one at a time. Stir in bourbon, orange zest, vanilla, salt, and toasted pecans. Pour filling into prepared crust. Bake pie until edges puff and center is just set, about 45–50 minutes. If the edges brown too much, carefully tent with aluminum foil. Remove from oven and let cool on rack for at least 1 hour. Serve pie warm or at room temperature with bourbon cream.

### For the bourbon whipped cream:
1 cup whipping cream, chilled
2 tablespoons sugar
1 tablespoon bourbon

Beat together whipping cream, sugar, and bourbon in a large bowl of an electric mixer until cream holds peaks.

# Bollo's
# Scones

*When we return for fall semester (wait, we're not students anymore) we plan on spending Saturday mornings at Bollo's, cozying up with a latte and one of their delicious pastries. The brown sugar gives these the most lovely flavor. We folded in dried cranberries and apricots and affectionately called them Hokie scones.*

Makes 12

2½ cups oats
½ cup brown sugar
1 tablespoon baking powder
½ teaspoon salt
1½ cups cold butter, cut into small pieces
1½ cups white pastry flour
1½ cups cake flour
¾ cup buttermilk
2 eggs
1 teaspoon vanilla extract
1½ cups dried fruit (cranberries, raisins, apricots, etc.)

Preheat oven to 350°F.

Place oats, brown sugar, baking powder, and salt in the bowl of a food processor or electric mixer. Before turning on, place cubed butter on top and then both flours. Process until the butter is the size of peas.

Whisk the eggs and buttermilk together with the vanilla in a medium bowl. Empty the oat mixture into a large bowl and pour the egg mixture over it.

Start tossing with fingers, working fast to get as much of the liquid evenly distributed with the dry ingredients. Add fruit and toss a little bit more. Take care to not overmix.

Wash and dry your hands. Dust your hands with a small amount of flour and press the dough into a ball. It should be firm but not sticky. If it is too sticky, add more cake flour. If it is too dry to hold together, add a little more buttermilk.

Working quickly, place the ball of dough on a cookie sheet and cut in half, put half on another sheet. Pat the dough into a circle and then cut into 6 triangles. Bake for 22 minutes, turning the pan around once, halfway through.

# Banana Walnut French Toast

*This recipe comes from Ranae Gillie, owner of Blacksburg's vegetarian restaurant, Gillie's. It's best made using high quality bread, which you may find in your local bakery. Gillie's makes this recipe from the bread baked down the street at Bollo's café, which Ranae also owns. The loaf should be sliced thick to absorb the custard without compromising the integrity of the bread.*

> "I could never decide between Gillie's French toast or the eggs Florentine so I always ordered both. I would joke to the waiter or waitress that I, of course, would not finish both. I always did. Whoopsies."
> —Krista

**Cook's Note:**
Gillie's cooks this in one very large skillet, but we used two because our skillet wasn't big enough to fit both the bananas and the bread.

Serves 4

1 whole loaf whole-wheat bread, cut into thick slices
2 large eggs
2 cups milk
1 teaspoon vanilla extract
2 teaspoons cinnamon
½ cup plus 1 tablespoon unsalted butter
1½ cups packed light brown sugar
½ cup chopped walnuts
3 medium bananas, sliced
confectioner's sugar, for serving

Place bread slices in a large casserole dish in an even layer. Beat eggs, milk, vanilla, and cinnamon in a medium bowl with a wire whisk until well blended. Pour egg mixture over the bread. Cover dish tightly and place in the refrigerator for 30–60 minutes.

Melt ½ cup butter in a medium frying pan or cast iron skillet on medium heat. Stir in the brown sugar and walnuts until the brown sugar is melted. Then add in the banana slices and cook for 1 minute, or until they are softened. Cover and keep warm until the bread is cooked.

Melt 1 tablespoon butter in a second frying pan. Place bread on the skillet in an even layer and cook, turning the bread only when it is golden brown on the bottom.

Cook second side until brown adding a little more butter to the pan if needed. Remove bread from pan and place on a platter, topping with the warm walnuts and bananas.

Add a sprinkle of confectioner's sugar for garnish.

# 622 North's
# Cucumber Cooler Martini

*Although 622 North is adored for its extensive wine list, the martinis are exquisite and change seasonally.*

Serves 1

¼ medium cucumber
2 ounces gin
¼ ounce sours
¼ ounce tonic
¼ ounce lemon-lime soda

Slice 3 paper-thin cucumber slices and set aside for later use. Slice cucumber in half lengthwise. Use a spoon to remove the seeds and any soft material. Slice in half lengthwise again and quarter. Place fresh cut cucumber quarters in shaker and add gin. Muddle cucumbers and gin. Strain into another shaker and discard muddled cucumbers. Add sours, tonic, lemon-lime soda, and ice into the shaker with gin. Shake and strain into a chilled martini glass. Float the 3 paper-thin slices of cucumber on top.

# Our Daily Bread's
# Almond Macarons

*Meeting owners Danielle and Thierry, a husband and wife team, was one of the most memorable and delightful moments during our research. Thierry was practically born in a bakery—in a small village in France—and before he married Danielle, gave her an ultimatum: "If you want to marry me, you need to know pastry." All it takes is one look in the long display case of beautiful pastries to know that they both know pastry.*

Makes 10

8 ounces almond paste
1 cup granulated sugar
2 egg whites (1.8 ounces) at room temperature

Preheat oven to 330°F.

Grease a baking sheet and piping bag.

Slowly mix almond paste and sugar in the bowl of an electric mixer. Slowly add egg white, a little at a time. Mix for approximately 10 minutes until the texture is smooth. The dough will be thick, like a paste.

Spoon dough into the piping bag and squeeze out round, uniform macaroons onto baking sheet.

Bake for 18 minutes (for smaller macaroons) or until golden. Remove from oven and allow to cool for 5 minutes on the baking sheet. Remove macaroons with a spatula and place on a rack to cool completely.

For the filling, let your imagination run wild. We suggest playing around with different types of jam, buttercream, or chocolate.

# The Farmhouse's
# Chocolate Chess Sundae Pie

*This charming and ultrapopular Christiansburg restaurant was built in the 1800s and has been serving the community since the 1960s—a perfect spot for a special occasion, a hot date, or when the 'rents are in town. The Farmhouse is best known for Southern cooking, juicy steaks, and indulgent desserts, like this silky chocolate pie.*

Makes 2

2 pie shells
½ pound butter
1 cup sugar
1 pound semisweet chocolate chips
3 eggs
1 tablespoon vanilla extract
1 cup milk
¾ cup flour
vanilla ice cream, for serving
chocolate syrup, for serving

Preheat oven to 325°F.

Dock the pie shells by poking holes in them with a fork to prevent bubbling. Bake for 4 minutes and set aside to cool.

Melt the butter, sugar, and chocolate chips in a double boiler, and whisk until smooth. Add the milk and whisk until smooth again.

Mix together the eggs and vanilla in the bowl of an electric mixer on medium speed for about 2 minutes. Add the flour and mix for 2 more minutes. Add the chocolate mixture and mix for 4 minutes. Pour into pie shells and bake for 25–30 minutes. Serve warm with vanilla ice cream and a drizzle of chocolate syrup.

# Peg Morse's
# Holiday Peppermint Ice Cream Sandwiches

*These delicious ice cream sandwiches are a holiday dream sensation, also great for parties and hungry college students during exams.*

Makes 12

2 pints peppermint ice cream
24 chocolate wafers
1 (16-ounce) container whipped topping, thawed
chocolate syrup, for decoration
crushed peppermint candy, for decoration

Prepare a surface with a large piece of parchment paper. Remove ice cream from freezer to soften just slightly, 3–5 minutes. Prepare a baking sheet that will fit in your freezer with another piece of parchment paper. Distribute 12 wafers on the baking sheet.

Remove slightly thawed ice cream from carton onto the first piece of parchment paper and mold with a rubber spatula into a 1-inch-thick rectangular slab. Working quickly, cut out 12 rounds with a 2-inch biscuit cutter. Alternatively, you may scoop out ice cream with a small ice cream scoop and place each scoop on a wafer. Place the remaining 12 wafers on top, making a sandwich. Place baking sheet in the freezer until they are hardened, about 30 minutes. Once frozen, place in freezer bags until early on the day you plan to serve the sandwiches.

On the day they are to be served, remove sandwiches from freezer and frost on all sides with whipped topping, leaving a "finger hold" if you wish. Drizzle chocolate syrup on top of each, sprinkle with candy chips, and return to freezer for at least 1 hour before serving.

"Peg was our HighTech sponsor, but really, she was more like our second mom. Just as any mother would, she put up with a lot. She drove us around, endured many long bus trips to our national competition in Daytona, and laughed along with each and every one of our jokes. Every December, we would look forward to the holiday party she hosted just for us. Wow, could she cook! Peg always made these peppermint ice cream sandwiches and I became extremely vocal about how much I loved them. At the Christmas party during my senior year, she made three extra sandwiches, just for me. I was so touched by her gesture, I had to eat all of them."

—Krista

# Next Door Bake Shop's
## Coconut Cream Cupcakes
## with Coconut Frosting

*I consider myself quite the cupcake connoisseur, so when I tell you that this recipe yields the lightest, fluffiest, most delicious cupcakes I've ever tasted, well, I'm not fooling around. The coconut flavor is perfection and the toasted coconut sprinkled on top really is nothing to mess around with. Oh ... my ... cupcake.*
*—Kris*

Makes 24

2½ cups cake flour
1 cup sugar
1 tablespoon baking powder
1 teaspoon Kosher salt
1 cup cream of coconut*
⅔ cup unsalted butter, softened
8 ounces sour cream
2 teaspoons vanilla extract
2 teaspoons coconut oil extract
2 tablespoons whole milk
3 eggs, lightly beaten

Preheat oven to 350°F.

Line 24 muffin cups with paper liners.

Sift together cake flour, sugar, and baking powder. Mix in salt.

Beat the cream of coconut, butter, and sour cream in the bowl of an electric mixer until well blended. Beat in vanilla and coconut extracts. Add flour mixture and milk alternately, in three additions, beginning and ending with the flour. Scrape down the side of the bowl as needed.

Add the eggs, one at a time, beating well after each addition. Scrape down the side of the bowl as needed.

Evenly fill the muffin cups two-thirds full and bake for 15–20 minutes or until golden brown and a toothpick inserted into a cupcake comes out clean. Do not overbake. Remove from oven and place on a cooling rack. Cool cupcakes completely before icing.

### For the frosting:
1 cup unsalted butter, at room temperature
2 teaspoons coconut oil extract
3 cups powdered sugar
⅓ cup cream of coconut
2 cups sweetened flaked coconut, lightly toasted, for garnish

Beat butter in a bowl of an electric mixer until smooth and fluffy. Add coconut oil extract. Add powdered sugar and cream of coconut alternately, beginning and ending with the powdered sugar. Beat on medium-low speed until blended, scraping down the side of the bowl as needed. Increase speed to medium-high and beat until light and fluffy.

Pipe frosting onto cooled cupcakes using a pastry bag fitted with large star tip. Sprinkle with toasted coconut.

*You may find this at a liquor store or the Latin/Hispanic section of your local grocery store

# The Beamer's
## Cola Cake

1 cup unsalted butter
1 cup cola beverage
2 tablespoons cocoa powder
1 cup mini marshmallows
2 cups flour
2 cups sugar
2 eggs, beaten
½ cup buttermilk
1 teaspoon baking soda
1 teaspoon vanilla extract

Preheat oven to 350°F.

Grease a 9 x 13-inch baking pan.

Place butter, cola, cocoa powder, and mini marshmallows in a medium saucepan on medium-high heat and bring to a boil. Lower the heat to medium. Continue to stir until the marshmallows have melted, about 5–7 minutes. Remove from heat and let cool slightly.

Combine flour and sugar in a large bowl. Set aside.

Combine eggs, buttermilk, baking soda, and vanilla in a small bowl. Set aside.

Add the hot cola mixture to the flour mixture and stir until just combined. Add the egg mixture to this and stir until incorporated.

Pour mixture into prepared pan and bake for 45 minutes, or until cake tester comes out clean.

**For the frosting:**
6 tablespoons cola
4 tablespoons cocoa powder
½ cup unsalted butter
3 cups powdered sugar

Place cola, cocoa, and butter in a medium saucepan on medium heat and bring to a boil. Turn off the heat and add powdered sugar. Mix together with a wire whisk to combine until lumps are removed. Mixture should be thick, but spreadable.

Pour hot mixture over the top of the warm cake and spread with a rubber spatula. Allow cake to cool for 20 minutes before serving; icing will harden slightly.

*This cake was a hit with all of my neighbors, so much so that I had to make it twice just to have a slice leftover for myself.*

*—Kris*

# Dr. Frank Conforti's
## Chocolate Chip Angel Food Cake

As a Human Nutrition, Foods, and Exercise major, Krista had the pleasure of attending Dr. Conforti's popular class "Food Selection and Preparation." Not only is Dr. Conforti hilarious, but his passion for cooking is contagious. His class covers both basic and advanced cooking techniques as well as the science of baking.

1 cup sifted cake flour
1½ cups confectioner's sugar
¼ cup mini semi-sweet chocolate chips
1½ cups egg whites, room temperature (about 12 large eggs)
1¼ teaspoons cream of tartar
¼ teaspoon salt
1½ teaspoons vanilla extract
½ teaspoon almond extract
¾ cup granulated sugar

Preheat oven to 375°F.

Set oven rack to the lowest position in the oven.

Sift together cake flour and confectioner's sugar 3 times over a sheet of waxed paper; set aside. Combine 2 tablespoons of the flour-sugar mixture with the chocolate chips in a small bowl and set aside.

Beat egg whites to foamy stage in the bowl of an electric mixer on high speed. Add cream of tartar, salt and vanilla and almond extracts. Continue beating the egg at high speed to the soft peak stage. Gradually add granulated sugar, 1 tablespoon at a time, until stiff and shiny peaks are formed. Check the meringue by rubbing a small amount between your fingers. If it feels gritty, continue beating. Check again after another minute.

Gradually sift the flour-confectioner's sugar mixture (in 3 additions) over the meringue and carefully fold in. Sprinkle the chocolate chips over the meringue and fold in. Carefully guide the batter into an ungreased 10-inch tube pan and bake 30–35 minutes or until the cake springs back when pressed.

Cool the cake upside down in the pan for at least 2 hours. Loosen the sides with a long slender spatula and remove. Top with chocolate glaze.

### For the chocolate glaze:
½ cup semisweet chocolate chips
¼ cup margarine, softened
2 tablespoons light corn syrup

Place chocolate chips, butter, and corn syrup in a small microwave-safe bowl. Heat in microwave on high power for 30 seconds. Remove from microwave and stir. Return to microwave if necessary and heat 15 seconds. Stir again. Continue heating and stirring if needed until glaze is smooth. With a thin spatula spread the glaze over the top of the cake, allowing it to drip down the sides.

# Maroon and Orange Cookies

*This is our take on the famous New York black and white cookie. This cookie is also just another excuse to add the beloved color combination to special (or random) occasions. As for the accessibility of the food coloring, we've used a combination of burgundy and red to achieve the perfect maroon.*

Makes 2 dozen

3 cups flour
½ teaspoon salt
¼ teaspoon baking soda
11 tablespoons unsalted butter, at room temperature
½ cup vegetable shortening
1⅓ cup sugar
2 eggs, at room temperature
2½ teaspoons vanilla extract
½ teaspoon lemon extract
2 teaspoons light corn syrup
⅓ cup sour cream

Preheat oven to 350°F.

Line baking sheet with parchment paper.

Stir together flour, salt, and baking soda in a medium bowl.

Blend together butter, shortening, and sugar in the bowl of an electric mixer on medium speed until well combined and fluffy, about 2 minutes. Add the eggs, vanilla and lemon extracts, and corn syrup, and continue to beat until combined. Beat in half of the flour mixture until blended. Beat in sour cream. Beat in remaining flour until just combined. Let dough stand 5 minutes to firm up.

Use a dry measuring cup to scoop out ¼ cup dough rounds. Place rounds on baking sheet about 3 inches apart. Grease your hands with a little oil and gently pat each round into a circle. Bake cookies on the middle rack of the oven for 10–13 minutes, or until lightly browned around the edges. Do not overbake.

Transfer the baking sheet to a wire cooling rack and let cookies stand 2 minutes. Using a spatula, transfer the cookies onto the wire rack and let stand until completely cooled.

*For the fondant:*
5 cups powdered sugar
¼ cup light corn syrup
1 teaspoon vanilla extract
½ teaspoon burgundy icing coloring
¼ teaspoon red icing coloring
¼ teaspoon orange icing coloring

Sift the powdered sugar into a large mixing bowl.

Combine ½ cup water and corn syrup in a small saucepan on medium-high heat and bring to a boil. Immediately remove from heat and carefully pour into the bowl of powdered sugar. Whisk to combine until completely smooth. Add vanilla.

Pour half of the icing into another mixing bowl. In a third bowl, add burgundy and red coloring and mix until evenly distributed. If needed, continue to add more of the red coloring to reach the shade you desire.

Add the orange coloring to the bowl of icing and mix until evenly distributed.

To ice the cookies with easy cleanup, place the cooling rack with the cookies on top onto the sheet pan. With a long, flat, metal spatula or butter knife, ice half of each cookie with the maroon icing. Ice the other half with the orange icing and let set until completely dry.

# Cramming for Finals
## Cookie Dough Cupcakes

*What kitchen wasn't stocked with the essentials for reading day? And by essentials, we mean cookie dough, cereal, and leftover pizza. This is a more civilized way to incorporate the midnight study time snack into your adult life, although really, Kris created this recipe to cram all of her favorite things into one dessert (cookie dough, cake, icing, sugar). It's all of the "fun" of cramming for finals without, you know, having to actually take them.*

1½ cups unsalted butter, at room temperature
1½ cups light brown sugar, packed
4 large eggs
2⅔ cups all-purpose flour
1 teaspoon baking powder
1 teaspoon baking soda
¼ teaspoon salt
1 cup milk
2 teaspoon vanilla extract
1 cup chocolate chips

Preheat oven to 350°F.

Line two cupcake pans with paper liners.

Combine the butter and brown sugar in the bowl of a stand mixer fitted with paddle attachment. Beat together on medium-high speed until light and fluffy.

Mix in the eggs one at a time, beating well after each addition and scraping down the sides of the bowl as needed.

Combine the flour, baking powder, baking soda, and salt in a medium bowl. Add the dry ingredients to the mixer bowl on low speed, alternating with the milk, beginning and ending with the dry ingredients. Blend in the vanilla. Fold in the chocolate chips with a spatula and mix by hand.

Divide the batter evenly between the prepared cupcake liners. Bake for 18–20 minutes until a toothpick inserted in the center comes out clean. Allow to cool in the pan for 5–10 minutes and then transfer to a wire rack to cool completely.

### For the filling:
4 tablespoons unsalted butter, at room temperature
6 tablespoons light brown sugar, firmly packed
1 cup plus 2 tablespoons all-purpose flour
7 ounces sweetened condensed milk
½ teaspoon vanilla extract
¼ cup mini semisweet chocolate chips

Combine the butter, sugar, and cream in the bowl of a stand mixer on medium-high speed until light and fluffy, about 2 minutes. Beat in the flour, sweetened condensed milk, and vanilla until incorporated and smooth. Stir in the chocolate chips.

To fill the cupcakes, cut a cone-shaped portion out of the center of each cupcake. Fill each hole with a chunk of the chilled cookie dough mixture. You can be generous with this mixture. We ended up with leftover dough (for eating, of course).

### For the frosting:
1½ cups (3 sticks) unsalted butter, at room temperature
¾ cup light brown sugar, packed
3½ cups confectioners' sugar
1 cup all-purpose flour
¾ teaspoon salt
3 tablespoons milk
2½ teaspoons vanilla extract

Place the butter and brown sugar in the bowl of a stand mixer fitted with the paddle attachment and beat until creamy. Mix in confectioner's sugar until smooth. Beat in flour and salt. Mix in milk and vanilla until smooth and well blended.

### For decoration:
tiny chocolate chip cookies
mini chocolate chips

Frost the filled cupcakes as desired, sprinkling with mini chocolate chips and top with mini chocolate chip cookies for decoration.

# Rail Brownies

*Unlike the actual drink these "Rail" brownies won't leave you with a headache the next day unless you get a sugar hangover from eating the entire pan in one sitting. So go ahead, indulge in as many as you wish. They are that good.*

**For the peanut butter topping:**
4 tablespoons unsalted butter, melted
½ cup powdered sugar
¾ cup crunchy (or smooth) peanut butter
¼ teaspoon salt
½ teaspoon vanilla extract

Whisk all ingredients together in a medium bowl until smooth. Set aside until ready to use.

**For the brownies:**
½ cup flour
⅓ cup cocoa powder
¼ teaspoon baking powder
¼ teaspoon salt
½ cup butter, melted
1 cup sugar
1 teaspoon vanilla extract
2 eggs
½ cup chocolate chips
handful of pretzel sticks

Preheat oven to 350°F.

Grease a 9-inch baking pan.

Stir together flour, cocoa, baking powder, and salt in a medium bowl and set aside.

Stir together butter, sugar, and vanilla in a large bowl. Add eggs and beat well. Add flour mixture to the butter mixture, and stir until it is well blended. Fold chocolate chips into batter.

Spread batter evenly in prepared pan. Pour peanut butter mix over brownie batter and make into swirls by gliding a knife through the batter. Arrange pretzel sticks parallel in the batter.

Bake approximately 25–30 minutes, or until a toothpick stuck in the batter comes out clean. Let cool entirely before taking out of the pan.

# Hokie Pokie Bars

½ cup unsalted butter, melted
1½ cups graham cracker crumbs
1 (14-ounce) can sweetened condensed milk
½ cup semisweet chocolate chips
½ cup colored chocolate-covered candies (maroon and orange ones, of course)
1⅓ cups sweetened flaked coconut
1 cup chopped nuts

Preheat oven to 350°F.

Grease an 8 x 8-inch-square baking pan with nonstick cooking spray.

Combine graham cracker crumbs and melted butter in a medium bowl. Press evenly into bottom of prepared pan.

Pour sweetened condensed milk over the crumb mixture. Layer evenly in the following order: chocolate chips, coconut, nuts, and chocolate covered candy. Press down firmly with a fork so the toppings are stuck into the condensed milk.

Bake 25 minutes or until the top is lightly browned. Cool for at least 30 minutes. Cut into bars. Store covered, at room temperature.

# Hokie Tartlets

*This recipe comes from our sorority sister, Christy Vega. These mini red velvet brownies with cream cheese icing will be the MVP of your next tailgate.*

Makes 24

1¼ cups flour
3 tablespoons unsweetened cocoa powder
¼ teaspoon salt
½ cup unsalted butter, at room temperature
¾ cup granulated sugar
¾ cup light brown sugar
2 eggs
2 tablespoons red food coloring

Preheat oven to 350°F.

Spray a mini muffin pan with nonstick cooking spray.

Whisk together flour, cocoa powder, and salt in a large bowl, and set aside.

Beat together butter and sugars until creamy. Add eggs, one at a time. Slowly add in food coloring. Add as much as you need to get a true maroon shade. Gradually add flour mixture into butter mixture, starting at a slow speed. Beat until just combined.

Add batter to pan using a small ice cream scoop and bake for 15–20 minutes, or until toothpick comes out clean. As soon as the brownies come out of the oven, make an indentation in each one, using the back of a small spoon.

### For the cream cheese icing:
6 ounces cream cheese, at room temperature
1 cup whipped cream topping
¼ cup powdered sugar
orange food coloring (or use 20 drops of yellow coloring with 9 drops of red coloring)

Beat the cream cheese in the bowl of an electric mixer until smooth. Add the whipped cream topping and the powdered sugar and beat until smooth. Slowly add the food coloring and mix until the color is even and the icing is smooth.

Add the icing to a piping bag fitted with a star tip. Pipe the icing into each cooled cup.

# Hokie Cupcakes

*Using Kris's grandmother's famous butter cake recipe, an elegant vanilla icing, and some amazing maroon and orange sprinkles that Krista found, these cupcakes are simply delicious and scream, "Hokie pride!"—if, of course, you ice them while wearing a jersey and humming the Virginia Tech "Fight Song."*

Makes 18–24

1 cup unsalted butter, softened
1½ cups sugar
3 large eggs
3 large egg yolks
1 tablespoon vanilla extract
3¼ cups flour
2½ teaspoons baking powder
¼ teaspoon salt
1¼ cups milk

Preheat oven to 350°F. Line 2 cupcake pans with paper liners.

Beat butter and sugar in the bowl of an electric mixer on medium-high speed until fluffy and pale yellow, about 4–5 minutes. Add eggs, then extra yolks, one at a time, beating well after each addition and scraping down sides of bowl as necessary. Beat in vanilla extract.

Mix together flour, baking powder, and salt in a separate medium bowl. Stir about a ⅓ of the flour mixture into butter mixture. Stir in ½ the milk until just blended. Stir in another ⅓ of the flour mixture and remaining milk, followed by remaining flour.

Bake for 25–30 minutes, or until a wooden skewer inserted in the center comes out clean. Cool on a rack in the pan for 10 minutes, remove cupcakes from pan, and cool completely before icing and decorating.

***For the icing:***
1 cup unsalted butter, softened
4 cups confectioner's sugar
3 to 4 tablespoons milk
1 teaspoon vanilla or almond extract

Beat together the butter and sugar in the bowl of an electric mixer on medium speed. Reduce the speed to low. Add in the milk and vanilla or almond extract, raise the speed back to medium, and beat for 3 minutes. If the icing is too thick, add in more milk, a tablespoon at a time, until icing reaches desired consistency. Ice cupcakes and top with maroon and orange sprinkles.

# Acknowledgments

To *Virginia Tech, you changed our lives and shaped us into who we are today—from the moment we received an acceptance letter to graduation day. You became our home, a place where we met some of our best friends and made memories to be cherished forever. We can only hope that this book does you justice.*

A Taste of Virginia Tech *would not have been possible without the support of many people--whose passion, excitement, and encouragement was inspiring.*

*Thank you to the members of the Virginia Tech community who graciously supported this project: Rick Johnson, Ted Faulkner, John Barrett, Rachel DeLauder, Steve Garnett, Dr. Edward Spencer, Tom Tillar, and Greg Fansler. Your stories gave this book life. To Chef Mark Bratton whose kindness was much appreciated. Thank you for going above and beyond and spending hours scaling down the popular West End Market recipes, giving students and alumni the opportunity to enjoy these great meals at home. To Chef Mark Moritz, thank you for contributing some amazing recipes, all while getting ready to launch a new dining facility. Virginia Tech is lucky to have you.*

*Thank you to all the restaurant owners, chefs, and individuals who contributed recipes. We were so inspired by all of your stories!*

To Naren, the CEO of Mascot Books, your enthusiasm for this book has been instrumental and you have been nothing short of awesome to work with. To the staff of Mascot Books, including Josh Taggert, Josh Patrick, and Laura Vasile, whose creative abilities and perfectionism exceeded our highest expectations.

To Laura Friedel, from Laura's Focus Photography, thank you so much for turning West End into a photo studio and making us look our best. Who knew that posing on tables and pretending to smash large burgers into our faces could be that much fun? You made our day- thank you for the beautiful shots.

To our amazing Tri-Delta interns: Katie Condes, Christina Wingfield, and Emily Cunningham, you three were essential to the completion of this project. Thank you so much for your hard work and enthusiasm.

## From Krista:

To my husband, Kevin, my favorite person and best friend, thank you for always encouraging me and for helping make this dream of mine a reality.

To Dad, thank you for your contagious entrepreneurial spirit and for always inspiring me to do what I love. Thank you for your love, guidance, and confidence in me.

To Mom, thank you for being my biggest cheerleader. I am so blessed to have you.

To my two sweet little boys, Liam and Jack, you've made my life complete.

Thank you to each of my "bonus parents"—Mom, Dad, Donna, and Bruce; my sweet sisters Blake and Erika; and Mimi, Granddad, Jeannie, and the rest of my amazing family. I love you so much.

Many friends have helped me along this journey. My thanks to Sara, my friend of 25 years, who essentially taught me how to write. It's great to have a friend who is also a dreamer. To my fellow HighTechs, Mich, Jen, Kathleen, Rash, Diva, Nadja, and Amanda, thank you for all the laughs, love, and support. To Kasey, Allison, and countless other friends (you all know who you are) who've gone on this journey with me: thank you!

*My thanks also to my Aunt Kim. I'm not sure words can explain what you mean to me. Thank you for being in my life.*

*To my cooking mentor, Joan Nathan, thank you for teaching me so much about the process of writing a cookbook.*

*To my amazing coauthor, Kris, it has been an absolute blast. Thank goodness we share the same inappropriate sense of humor.*

*"De gustibus non est disputantum" (There is no disputing taste)*

## From Kris:

*To my husband, Peter, voor altijd. You are my rock. Go big or go home, right?*

*Dad, thank you for always encouraging me to be a dreamer. Mom, I love you more. Carla, I am forever grateful for our deep (crazy sister) bond. David, I love you as if you were mine. Ollie, I hope to instill in you my passion for cooking, or at least get you hooked on peanut butter.*

*To the Schoels, my number-one European fans, thank you for welcoming me into your family with open arms and always tasting every crazy concoction I made.*

*To all of the girls, thank you. Life wouldn't be the same without you. I remember the moment we all met as awkward freshmen in the sorority house, just trying to find our place.*

*To Krista, my partner in crime, I would write something totally cheesy and sentimental, but humor is more our style. I am so excited I got to work with you on this book and we share the same taste in, well, pretty much everything. Can you believe we met via our mutual love for Britney? Dreams.*

*Cooking is one of the ways I show love and affection. I can only hope that this book shows that to all of you.*

# Index

## Sweets, Treats, Hokie-Inspired Eats